EXTENDED SIMILES

JENNY JOSEPH

EXTENDED SIMILES

BLOODAXE BOOKS

ISBN: 1 85224 302 3

First published 1997 by
Bloodaxe Books Ltd,
P.O. Box 1SN,
Newcastle upon Tyne NE99 1SN.

Bloodaxe Books Ltd acknowledges
the financial assistance of Northern Arts.

Cover printing by J. Thomson Colour Printers Ltd, Glasgow.

Printed in Great Britain by
Cromwell Press Ltd, Broughton Gifford, Melksham, Wiltshire.

Acknowledgements

Eight of these pieces were published by Enitharmon Press in 1991 under the title *Beached Boats* with photographs by Robert Mitchell in a folio edition, and twenty in a book of that name. Acknowledgements are due to the editors of the following publications where some of these pieces have also appeared: *Argo, Aquarius, Getting a Word in Edgeways*, edited and published by Bryan Ricketts (1997), *Oxford Magazine, Poetry Book Society Anthology 1986/87*, edited by Jonathan Barker (PBS/Hutchinson, 1986), *Poetry Book Society Anthology 1988-1989*, edited by David Constantine (PBS/Hutchinson, 1988), *Poetry Review. The Rhythm of Our Days*, edited by Veronica Green (Cambridge University Press, 1991) and *South West Arts magazine*.

The extracts from the introduction to *Lao Tzu: Tao Te Ching*, translated by D.C. Lau (Penguin Classics, 1963), and *The Periodic Table* by Primo Levi, translated by Raymond Rosenthal (Michael Joseph, 1985; English translation copyright © 1984 by Schocken Books Inc, Italian text copyright © 1975 Giulio Einaudi editore. s.p.a. Torino), are reproduced by permission of Penguin Books Ltd.

The preface also includes extracts from the following: D.F. McKenzie's *Bibliography and the Sociology of Texts*, from his 1985 Panizzi lecture, published by the British Library in 1986; Basil Willey's *The Seventeenth-Century Background* (Chatto & Windus, 1950); 'The Garden of Anecdotes', from *Ancient Chinese Fables* (Foreign Languages Press, Beijing, 1981); George Steiner's *After Babel*, second edition (Oxford University Press, 1992).

The cover painting by Nina Carroll was photographed by Robert Mitchell.

Contents

EXTENDED SIMILES

Preface

In some few cases the verses were turned into prose and printed as such, it having been unanticipated at that time that they might see the light.

THOMAS HARDY: Preface to *Wessex Poems* (1898)

I wanted to penetrate the Firebird and Aleko without illustrating them, without copying anything. I don't want to represent anything. I want the colour to play and speak alone. There is no equivalent between the world in which we live and the world we enter in this way.

MARC CHAGALL: Letter to Jacques Lassaigne

...as Dreams are the Fancies of those that sleep, so Fancies are but the Dreams of men awake. And these Fanices by day, as those Dreams by night, will vary and change with the weather and present temper of the Body;

So those that have only a fiery Enthusiastick acknowledgement of God; change of diet, feculent old age, or some present damps of Melancholy, will as confidently represent to their Phansy that there is no God, as ever it was represented that there is one. And then having lost the use of their more noble Faculties of Reason and Understanding, they must according to the course of Nature be as bold Atheists now, as they were before confident Enthusiasts.

...And the Enthusiast's bodily dictating the careless ravings of his own tumultuous Phansy for undeniable Principles of Divine knowledge, confirms the Atheist that the whole business of Religion and Notion of God is nothing but a troublesome fit of over-curious Melancholy

...there being that near alliance and mutuall correspondence betwixt these two enormous distempers of the Mind, Atheism and Enthusiasm.

HENRY MORE: *A brief discourse of the Nature Causes Kindes and Cure of Enthusiasm* (1656)

Scholastic thought was predominantly metaphysical: it was concerned, that is to say, with Being and Essence, Cause and End. It existed to give answers to the questions that children ask, but which the adult consciousness first dismisses as unanswerable and then forgets – questions taking the form of 'Why?' 'Whence?' 'What is it made of?' and 'Who made it or put it there?'....
....We must ask 'What?' 'Whence?' and 'Why?'; we differ from St Thomas mainly in having no direct replies to give. All we can do is reply in terms of 'As If'; 'live according to the best hypotheses (whatever they may be)', thus runs our reply to the questioner, 'live thus, and see if you can live the hypothesis into "truths" (truths for yourself, that is)'.

BASIL WILLEY: *The Seventeenth-Century Background*

Good is as visible as green.

JOHN DONNE: 'Communitie'

Traditionally, a map has rarely shown what anyone can see: its relation to reality is like that of words to the world – almost entirely arbitrary, not mimetic. Just as we see a landscape because we have already named its parts and look for what we know – for 'valley, rock and hill' – so maps take on meaning by virtue of the conventional understanding given to signs and their structure in a particular text. The most primitive expressions of spatial relationships in a map is more symbolic than representational since it must involve scale and omission of detail...maps are not subject-specific any more than books, photographs and films are. Nor are they material-specific.

D.F. MCKENZIE: *Bibliography and the Sociology of Texts*

His office was indulgently to fit
Actives to passives. Correspondency
Only his subject was.

JOHN DONNE: 'Love's Deitie'

There is no name that is applicable to the *tao* because language is
totally inadequate for such a purpose...The difficulty of finding
appropriate language to describe the *tao* lies in the fact that although
the *tao* is conceived of as that which is responsible for the creation
as well as the support of the universe, yet the description the Taoist
aimed at was a description in terms of tangible qualities as though
the *tao* were a concrete thing...

...Thus we can see that no term can be applied to the *tao* because
all terms are specific, and the specific (if applied to the *tao*) will
impose a limitation on the range of its function. And the *tao* that
is limited in its function can no longer serve as the *tao* that sus-
tains the manifold universe.

D.C. LAU: Introduction to *Lao Tzu*

Since finding out what something is is largely a matter of discover-
ing what it is like, the most impressive contribution to the growth
of intelligibility [about the processes which constitute health] has
been made by the application of suggestive metaphors.

JONATHAN MILLER: *The Body in Question*

And God having usually made this world to be a mappe and shadow of the spirituall estate of the soules of man: therefore give me leave for the better discerning of things in this kind; learne wee to discerne the signes of our owne times; for the signes of the weather in which our Saviour makes his comparison, and there are certain signes and seasons of the weather to which a man may compare the estate of his owne time and season.

JOHN COTTON: Sermon
('The wickeds craft to insnare Gods people described')

There's something about the worm that the human being can relate to.

from a BBC radio programme about raising worms
by banging on the surface of the soil

Who sweeps a room as for Thy laws...

GEORGE HERBERT: 'The Elixir'

We cannot cage the minute
Within its nets of gold

LOUIS MACNEICE: 'The Sunlight on the Garden'

Gaia – one shape of many names
Proteus – the opposite

Oil paint is the perfect analogue for the density of the phenomenal world.

'Hui Zi is forever using parables,' complained someone to the Prince of Liang. 'If you, Sire, forbid him to speak in parables, he won't be able to make his meaning clear.'

The Prince agreed with the man.

The next day the Prince saw Hui Zi.

'From now on,' he said, 'kindly talk in a straightforward manner, and not in parables.'

'Suppose there were a man who did not know what a catapult is,' replied Hui Zi. 'If he asked you what it looked like, and you told him it looked just like a catapult, would he understand what you meant?'

'Of course not,' answered the Prince.

'But suppose you told him that a catapult looks something like a bow and that it is made of bamboo – wouldn't he understand you better?'

'Yes, that would be clearer,' admitted the Prince.

'We compare something a man does not know with something he does know in order to help him understand it,' said Hui Zi. 'If you won't let me use parables, how can I make things clear to you?'

The Prince agreed that he was right.

FROM 'The Garden of Anecdotes'

Praxis goes ahead, must go ahead *as if*; theory has no licence to do so.

GEORGE STEINER: *After Babel*

The atom we are speaking of, accompanied by its two satellites which maintained it in a gaseous state, was therefore borne by the wind along a row of vines in the year 1848. It had the good fortune to brush against a leaf, penetrate it, and be nailed there by a ray of the sun. If my language here becomes imprecise and allusive, it is not only because of my ignorance: this decisive event, this instantaneous work *a tre* – of carbon dioxide, the light, and the vegetal greenery – has not yet been described in definitive terms, and perhaps it will not be for a long time to come, so different is it from that other "organic" chemistry which is the cumbersome, slow and ponderous work of man; and yet this refined, minute and quick-witted chemistry was "invented" two or three billion years ago by our silent sisters, the plants, which do not experiment and do not discuss, and whose temperature is identical to that of the environment in which they live. If to comprehend is the same as forming an image, we will never form an image of a happening whose scale is a millionth of a millimetre, whose rhythm is a millionth of a second, and whose protagonists are in their essence invisible. Every verbal description must be adequate, and one will be as good as the next, so let us settle for the following description.

Our atom of carbon enters the leaf, colliding with other innumerable (but here useless) molecules of nitrogen and oxygen. It adheres to a large and complicated molecule that activates it, and simultaneously receives the decisive message from the sky, in the flashing form of a packet of solar light; in an instant, like an insect caught by a spider, it is separated from its oxygen, combined with hydrogen and (one thinks) phosphorus, and finally inserted in a chain, whether long or short does not matter, but it is the chain of life. All this happens swiftly, in silence, at the temperature and pressure of the atmosphere, and gratis: dear colleagues, when we learn to do likewise we will be *sicut Deus*...

...It is possible to demonstrate that this completely arbitrary story is nevertheless true. I could tell innumerable other stories, and they would all be true: all literally true, in the nature of the transitions, in their order and their data. The number of atoms is so great that one could always be found whose story coincides with any capriciously invented story. I could recount an endless number of stories about carbon atoms that become colours or perfumes in flowers; of others which, from tiny algae to small crustaceans to fish, gradually return as carbon dioxide to the waters of the sea, in a perpetual, frightening round-dance of life and death, in which every devourer is immediately devoured; of others which instead attain a decorous semi-eternity in the yellowed pages of some archival document, or the canvas of a famous painter; or those to which fell the privilege of forming part of a grain of pollen and left their fossil imprint in the rocks for our curiosity; of others still that descended to become part of the mysterious shape-messengers of the human seed, and participated in the subtle process of division, duplication and fusion from which each of us is born. Instead, I will tell just one more story, the most secret, and I will tell it with the humility and restraint of him who knows from the start that his theme is desperate, his means feeble, and the trade of clothing facts in words is bound by its very nature to fail.

It is again among us, in a glass of milk. It is inserted in a very complex long chain, yet such that almost all of its links are acceptable to the human body. It is swallowed; and since every living structure harbours a savage distrust toward every contribution of any material of living origin, the chain is meticulously broken apart and the fragments, one by one, are accepted or rejected. One, the one that concerns us, crosses the intestinal threshold and enters the bloodstream: it migrates, knocks at the door of a nerve cell, enters, and supplants the carbon which was part of it. This cell belongs to a brain, and it is my brain, the brain of the me who is writing; and the cell in question, and within it the atom in question, is in charge of my writing, in a gigantic miniscule game which nobody has yet described. It is that which at this instant, issuing out of a labyrinthine tangle of yesses and nos, makes my hand run along a certain path on the paper, mark it with these volutes that are signs: a double snap, up and down, between two levels of energy, guides this hand of mine to impress on the paper this dot, here, this one.

PRIMO LEVI: from 'Carbon', *The Periodic Table*

Castles in the sand

A man scoops the sand up into a pile. The long sea rollers run continuously from the horizon. He scoops it into a pile and carves it as if it were rock. We see the grains and the ease of the little knife he uses so it is still sand though it is becoming a wall, a castle, and carved and shaped as if from rock.

But it is a picture. The camera shows us windows, arches, buttresses, rising quickly formed at once. It perhaps took hours. The walled cities out of rock took years. That is the pleasure of toys. The blancmange cat, dolls' house life, the model lighthouse, there is not the tedious and perpetual push of recalcitrant material, the time it takes for the blood to circulate, the years for peat to form. The sands of the Yang-tse took centuries to be pressed into rock. Thought, imagination, is in a different time-scheme from getting across the town, wringing out the washing, taking a boat out on the river, processing the picture, placing the page. Getting clothes on and putting a girdle round the earth happen at the same moment in the morning but inhabit utterly separate times. Winged thought indeed.

The building of sand is taking shape, has become the battlements of a city, for the camera moves and we are as if on a cliff. Placing its object the positioning of the shot has placed us, has put us high up in the sea air looking down the cliff-like side of this immense bastion as if into a dark narrow alley far below. How massively they built in those days. You think of the great cliff-sided well-like courts, the bluff sides of tall tenements in Edinburgh down flights of steps, you look up at the patch of sky and are dizzy, hemmed in by cliff-like man-made structures out of the rock of Edinburgh, as if hewn. Medieval castles perched above the abyss rise from the crags of the Rhine gorge as if spurs of rock have grown fairy-tale pinnacles as a tree's branch becomes complicated with leaves.

Then we are further off. It is as if we have been moved back and we then approach it from a distance, the sea in relation, the light on the shore which the waves are running up and the finished structure on the beach as if in a frame. The hands that we saw close up scraping and flicking, the little blade touching up the inside of the miniature arch, are now in proportion to the man who stands beside the castle he has made. We have moved back and what we now see is a man who takes a picture. His hands hold a camera. He takes a picture of the castle and we see the blank paper he pulls out as if we were watching it with him. A picture of the structure on the beach beside the sea materialises on the paper and becomes clearer and behind the edges of the picture of the photo is the sea-shore scene, which is itself a picture.

And as the picture of the photograph makes it look as if it's becoming clearer so the castle that the man has actually built begins to be knocked down by the sea and the wind, or rather, looking at the television screen as if we were looking through a window on to a scene, it seems as if there had been a building that a man had taken a picture of and that the sea and the wind destroyed, as if there were a sea and a wind, as if it was sand as if it was rock as if it was carved into the likeness of a huge complicated rabbit-warren of a building as fancy as Milan cathedral as if it was destructible as sand again. Little grains. It was made of little grains. The focus shifts. The titles move up through the oncoming breakers. They say that the picture, what we see, is made up of black and white grains, you see them when things are out of focus.

The film was called *Châteaux de Sable*. A castle as if it were of sand. Sand as if it were a castle. A picture as if it were a castle. *Châteaux de sable* as we should say sandcastles. But what a thing is like is never the same as what it is. Sandcastle and château de sable are not quite the same, châteaux de sable is like Châteaux en Espagne or as we say in English: castles in the air – of sand, of air, as if.

Barley sugar sun

We can only describe something by describing something else. If I used the word sun to describe the sun to someone who had never seen it, what use would that be?

So if I want to make you see this sun I see so clear and round in the western sky, a translucent filled-in globe, not a dazzle of criss-crossing diamond-white spikes, I might say it is orange like those dark-orange barley sugars partly sucked through of the sort that was convex and of a reddish orange. Of course, you who had both seen the sun and also held between forefinger and thumb the sweet from your mouth to see how round it still was, and wondered that it was so translucent and gleaming when before it was solid and floury, would know that I did not mean you to think of the stickiness of a sucked barley-sugar or of the sharpness of the thin edge or its hardness or splinteriness when bitten or its taste, but the golden light that filled it and the curve of its rim.

The only word for sky is sky, and anything else that tells us about it is describing something else: *winter* sky, *blue* sky, sky*wards*, *in the* sky, *cloudy stormy cold* sky – but now it is clear, fading after a hot day and, at a stage after the round of the sun is no more visible but only the light from it, there will be a point where it becomes the darkest blue again; a blue without light, a velvet darkness of a warm night.

And if you were a messy child of the sort that teachers think 'disgusting' you may have learnt more about the barley sugar than its hardness in your mouth and sticky sweetness by taking it out of your mouth and holding it up to the light and saying, 'It looks like the sun.' The sun can only be the sun but it looks like something else, a ball on fire, a disc, the streaks of melting golden syrup in hot porridge when it is sinking in flocked cloud, liquid gold. The sun is like a barley sugar when the barley sugar is like the sun. $x = y$ where y is x.

A more precise description – the only true one – would be that the sun is 864,000 miles across, that its mean distance from the earth is 93,003,000 miles, its surface 12,000 times that of the earth, its volume 1,300,000 times, but its density being $1/4$ that of the earth, its mass is only 332,000 times as great.

But we cannot thereby see the sun, we cannot make another know the sun we have seen and felt, what the sun is to us, not to its measuring maker.

He who the truth would know
About about about must go.

And now as I leave you and go on the coach, the lulling journey across the countryside, we pass the filled-in quarries. It is another day, a dull and stormy morning with fitful gleams of sun when the tossed clouds clear it now and then. As we pass the lake made out of the old quarries one shaft strikes it. The light on the water seems dead, on the surface only, coming only from the top rind, no source far off waking the life within, no illumination. The water is like the crinkled glass in bathroom windows where the ridge of the stamped flower or star pattern scintillates with the light behind the glass – thick glass light reflected from a dense surface, lighting up nothing, no joy, no warmth in it.

And soon we will come to the corner where from a group of bushes by the highway always rises up a dense flock of birds as the coach swings round. Perhaps this time I shall see in time the branches covered as if with leaves before their flight denudes them, and so tell what they are. They go up suddenly a dense mass, like a puff of dust in a spurt, like leaves shaken from the hedge by one blast of air, but all at once. I do not know what bush it is nor what the birds are, we go by too quickly. I only notice that it happens each time on that corner.

O nameless flocks of birds, maybe out there beyond the glass you sing more sweetly than the proverbial swallow. You rush up, you pass and because I cannot net you with a name you are only what you are for this moment, a sudden flight of many black bits. You have no place feeding the life ahead of me and no past, as do the legendary nightingale and the recognisable robin. You are only at this corner, in this moment. You throw your pattern on the air as you go but the traces disappear with your passage. I cannot describe you to my friend, for to see your likeness I have to know what you are: for we can only say something is like something if we know what it is like, we know what it is.

Hot and cold taps

We warned you not to put your hand under the hot tap – 'Hot-hot. Very hot. Burn you. Hurty,' we said but you had already managed to turn the tap and screamed as the water gushed over the back of your hand while we were shouting, 'No. Hot.'

It was the cold tap you had turned, though.

If we had not warned, not put fear into your nerves, and put that fear into a word, would you have been burnt by the icy water, soft hand all red, the word made fire?

The boy in the desert had a circle drawn round him and was told that if he crossed that indentation – a shallow mark made scrubbily with a stick – he would die, serpents would rise up, he could not pass, as if it was a circle of petrol in the sand lit to defeat a scorpion.

You could not have dragged that haunted boy over the dire embargo made with words. His joints were locked with will power – the word made iron. Nothing for him was a substitute, standing for, as if; it was thing, absolute. He could not move his foot.

We inculcate, it is said, with a word: ('Hot') fear, ('nasty') recoil. Yet we are only supplying words for what you want desperately to name.

For the extremes, the rays at each end of the spectrum, the sounds at pitches below and above what humans can hear, we cannot give you words. And so gradually your world will become only that lighted area we tame (name) for you where hot and cold should be separate. For you now everything is prime, what it is. Burn is burn. Your mother is what she is. No 'as if' in your world – effects not causes. You will go on trying things with your hands until you get some approximating sound to lasso them in, leaving the undefined edges unpursued, as a path which has no signpost may go unwalked and get grown over. There is so much of the brightly lit here and now to encompass;

as if we were on a platform, sitting round a table, laid for dinner and the dinner table, place mats, cutlery, napery, cruet, and the apron stage, is lit, all our actions are in the light. Beyond the edge, in the pit, even up by the lights under the dome whence the beam comes, is nothing because it is dark. The steep step from the lighted stage is like a cliff-side on a moonless night.

It is not on our arranged tableau but in the shock where extremes meet, where the current jumps round the almost joined-up circlet, that there are iced suns, that you get a dazzle from sightlessness, a burn off the freeze.

FROM *The Rambler* VIII
Saturday 14 April 1750. S. JOHNSON

That the soul always exerts her peculiar powers, with greater or less force, is very probable, though the common occasions of our present condition require but a small part of that incessant cogitation; and by the natural frame of our bodies, and general combination of the world, we are so frequently condemned to inactivity, that as through all our time we are thinking, so for a great part of our time we can only think.

Lest a power so restless should be either unprofitably or hurtfully employed, and the superfluities of intellect run to waste, it is no vain speculation to consider how we may govern our thoughts, restrain them from irregular motions, or confine them from boundless dissipation.

How the understanding is best conducted to the knowledge of science, by what steps it is to be led forward in its pursuit, how it is to be cured of its defects, and habituated to new studies, has been the enquiry of many acute and learned men, whose observations I shall not either adopt or censure; my purpose being to consider the moral discipline of the mind, and to promote the increase of virtue rather than of learning.

This inquiry seems to have been neglected for want of remembering that all action has its origin in the mind, and that therefore to suffer the thoughts to be vitiated is to poison the fountains of morality; irregular desires will produce licentious practices; what men allow themselves to wish they will soon believe, and will be at last incited to execute what they please themselves with contriving.

The sun in cloud

The clear round of the sun now shone on the back of the cloud it was beneath, lighting up cloud turrets and rocks, plains and uplands going back in depth with a wonderful perspective. You could travel that country you felt. The light bulged between bars of cloud that began to cross the sun rapidly. As it sank behind cloud it took its hidden secret life to itself, peeping out, travelling on; you couldn't quite tell where it was, it was a thinning of the veils that moved across it, an edging with brightness to the clouds that spread over it; it was known to be there, not seen. It emerged a squashed shape, then cleared the cloud and was whole again. Then it dispersed into streaks which were sometimes cloud-obfuscated, sometimes clear.

As the light dims it loses its power as the focal point for all we look at, its power to draw us always to look at it and see everything by its light.

And your smile of happiness, and your love, lighted everything in my world so I felt the whole place was a bright inviting country, and all we would do – suffer and travail across, – lit with it, interesting, worth it.

Jewelled was the valley

Jewelled was the valley, thick with sparkles of light, and then, higher up unevenly scattered over the dark mass of the wooded hill. At the densest dark, up near the imperceptible line where dark bulk became dark space, were one or two far single points, as if a single pearl had been dropped here and there from a hand clutching a broken necklace, no longer able to keep them all in before releasing them into the basket it was moving over.

Two walkers climbed up out from the sparkled valley over the dark edge which was backed by soft cloud, and up again and out on to the high hidden road.

'...like sun upon the face'

All we know is the physical, the sun, the light on water, the wind stirring the water, the brightness of colour strengthening through the slanting spring rain. How can I describe love except to say it is like the water beginning to move a little under a sudden push of air, how your goodness but that it is the light rippling across, making the colours strong, and the chords come down in the major again?

How say there is no tangible tip in the visible world that is not elsewhere much more, much stronger, without saying that the elusiveness of the physical is like afternoon fading gradually from a primrose-yellow wall – you are never quite sure when the sunlight has gone or how, or when the yellow you see is the paint on the wall; without saying that the furniture is there all through the night when we don't see it, leading its life unnoticed, that if I drop a penny in the bucket at the fair it will never cover the (sixpence it used to be) coin on the bottom because incalculable layers of water will take it this way that way sidling through byways of thought.

Even to say that the physical is all we know but that we must live in a state where it is unreachable because it is attached, wrapped round, enmeshed, grown from things we cannot know as physical, even to say this I need to know a bucket, surface of water, pennies, a child squatting, its soft grimy hand opening to drop its coin, seeing only the rim of the bucket and across it at most the stamped-out grass crowded with feet and legs up to the calves.

Oscar Wilde said that 'it is in the brain that the rose is red, the apple odorous, the lark sings'. He had seen flowers, he had been in gardens.

So if I am to be warmed by the sun, let your loving face light up the room for me; though you are as far as the sun that throws our sunshine on the wall, if I can think of you it is as if you were here.

FROM *The Rambler* VIII *(cont.)*

If the most active and industrious of mankind was able, at the close of life, to recollect distinctly his past moments, and distribute them, in a regular account, according to the manner in which they have been spent, it is scarcely to be imagined how few would be marked out to the mind by any permanent or visible effects, how small a proportion his real action would bear to his continued vacuity, and how many interstitial spaces unfilled, even in the most tumultuous hurries of business, and the most eager vehemence of pursuit. It is said by modern philosophers that not only the great globes of matter are thinly scattered through the universe, but the hardest bodies are so porous, that, if all matter were compressed to perfect solidity, it might be contained in a cube of a few feet. In like manner, if all the employment of life were crowded into the time which it really occupied, perhaps a few weeks, days, or hours, would be sufficient for its accomplishment, so far as the mind was engaged in the performance. For such is the inequality of our corporeal to our intellectual faculties, that we contrive in minutes what we execute in years, and the soul often stands an idle spectator of the labour of the hands and expedition of the feet.

Blackbird's whistle

Blackbird, you are somewhere I can't see. Your liquid whistle echoes in the space bounded by the tall beeches at the bottom of the field, the cluster of houses away over open gardens to the left. I wait while a tit see-saws its song for you to begin again so that I might trace the sound to where you are. Now I see the tit fly across on to the beech trunk, quiet for a moment yet I know he's there because I can now see him although he is pretty well camouflaged, but I have traced his coming there and can see him still. Strange this feeling that unless we can see the bird who sings, see the bird singing, we do not quite know he is there, who it is who sings. I can see the crows, they are always only too visible and present. But it is your lovely song I want to trace, to reach, although it is the sound of it that is to me the precious thing and not as with the robin and wren the neat and charming flitter of themselves as well as their voice.

Promised land

The embankment fell away on the left as I drove and the morning sun shone on the plain now revealed. It spread out to a very far horizon. The road which cut round the slope of the higher land on the southern edge of the plain curved to the right, so that only by glimpses over my shoulder could I see into this green and golden space stretching on my left hand. Indeed it was a relief that the road bent that way otherwise the rising sun would have beamed into my eyes blinding me altogether.

It was not a flat dull plain but varied ground down there, with clusters of woods and slopes and bars of mist in gently-folded valleys. I wanted to stop and take in the golden land, the desired, the far isle suddenly materialised, just over there, here, now spread out down below on my left, more of it opening up with every turn of the wheels. But the most I could do was snatch an occasional sight, take a little gasp or two as if I was in it, breathing in the fresh and lovely morning sun-caressed blue and green-refreshed air. For I had to keep my eye very continuously on the road, on the traffic a little ahead, on that hoving up on my wing, watching all the while the situation several ahead, several behind, on each side too, for I was driving (and could not slack) at a consistently and quite fast speed in the middle lane. It was no good trying to concentrate on the remembering, the marking, the noting of the lovely land, the haven, the good place suddenly manifest there, quite simply there, turned up just like any next bit on an ordinary journey. I was in that stream of traffic and everything must cease to exist but manoeuvring it – a flick of the eye to the driver passing on the right, a little spurt to get clear of the three racing lorries, a slowing down and falling back in to the left to let a coach, bearing down, the bully of the road, pass. (Rather have him in front than behind me, that one.) A sudden decision, based on second by second qualifications of the situation, to sail out and pass that bunch and then a steadying down now, past the junctions.

Now I found myself absorbed in the cinematograph run-through of the surface of the mind: conversations, poses, settling this score by never-to-be-actualised dramatisation, doing accounts, arranging the lists for the tournament of the day ahead, so that when something needed my attention on the road, a sudden appearance of cars in front, to be passed, to be slowed down for, to be slid back from, to be joined, I felt alarm that my attention had wandered from the yards of tarmac, from the driving. I thought if questioned I would not be able to recall the details of that last stretch of road at all, but would have, had it been necessary. My eyes had been doing the watching for me. Only my inner eye had been off elsewhere.

So that some time on, near journey's end and when so many little things had been noticed and acted on, when so much had at the same time been passing through my mind, I felt it was a long time ago, way back in the early morning start, that that beautiful stretch of land had revealed itself, the lovely sight spreading itself for all to see.

And perhaps if we had been travelling over the other side of the plain, working our way through it, the road we in fact were on, and these curving haunches of land sweeping up to a crown of trees, might themselves have seemed the desirable, the El Dorado, the promise, and what had to me on my route been the alluring distance then would have been the familiar, the practical, the business we must attend to with only quick glances across.

We had to concentrate on the road, the business of driving. But it was only because we were going that road that we saw it, that plain, with the sun shining out of a sky where the misty coverings were being gathered into high light puffy white bunches of cloud far away, where the colours and the shades were strengthening as the light poured, where was invitation, solace, high spiritedness, adventure.

Catching the moment

In an interview at the age of ninety Sir Geoffrey Keynes was asked how he had managed to achieve so much in the world of literary scholarship as well as carrying on his duties as a busy doctor, cultivating his beautiful garden, up to show standards, still clipping his hedges himself – for wasn't he halfway up a ladder when the interviewer arrived? – as well as having time for a wide circle of friends. He said the only trick he had with time was 'Do it (whatever it is) now.'

When the bird lands on the wire, the raindrop's moment of suspension is annihilated.

The shaft of sunlight laying, as if someone is waiting, on the top landing late afternoon, in the quiet house, is eclipsed when the door to the attic, whose one-paned window looks to the west, is closed.

Once the animal chases helter-skelter into the bushes, the outline of the dog with its paws upheld, tail straight nose to the wind one tense line, is expunged in a flash; as the energy in the fur-bulked hump of the cat on the wall as it concentrates on watching is dispersed when it is shooed away and becomes a fleeing streak, all limbs.

As soon as the poised dancer leaps to the right, the twirl to the left must be foregone. If the leap is initiated to end in a bird shape, head back on partner's breast, covering the stage with the short anxious patter of a wood animal is out of the question then. The giving gesture from clench at heart to open-armed offer can only be flung at one time to one person. Which side are we to let our weight come down on, which tempo join in on, shall we start now or sink back to get there later? But to stand still and do nothing – that also is a decision which excludes the others.

The expectancy of the parted lips is closed off by the kiss.

If you are to use the moment you must sacrifice it. Do it 'now' – which now, whose now? The now of the bird landing on the jewelled clothes line, or the drop that catches the light? The position of dog, of dancer, is only held because it is the base for the next that will destroy it. 'The only way to keep a dream is not to live it' a writer said, talking of the Promised Land; and surely Time eats not its children but its progenitors.

Arthur Koestler said that the time he was immured in prison in Spain seemed to stretch endlessly because nothing whatsoever happened in it, but that in retrospect those heavy hours were as if passed in a flash because there was nothing to mark their passage. Empty, they had vanished totally, more lost even than if he had slept away his life there.

As I write this in another place, another time to all the above circumstances, I cannot watch what is happening to the last edge of light round the thickening cloud, I cannot follow with my eyes every position of the horses as they move up the road, now collecting on the lush verge to browse, now spreading across the road as if in sociable congress which halts the cars. I can only notice afterwards that the sky has been uniformly overcast, the dusk spread evenly, that the road being empty the horses must have reached their destination. But even if I had taken my eyes off sky and road and horses for not one second, the night would have drawn over, the road emptied, the horses gone.

Arresting the sequential

'Closing in, closing in on the prey.' The not very appropriate words surfaced in his head, wide of the mark but siphoning off excitement. He knew what he meant. He was standing very still looking at a flower in a pot.

Surely if you stay still and concentrate enough you could catch the action. There must be some point when if you stayed there you could see it move, for it must move to go from closed to open. There was a lot of space between the expectant breath of the bud and the open flower. Surely you could catch it if you concentrated;

and surely if you stare hard enough without letting your mind wander away from your eyes, stop everything but the surface of your eyes, in the *trompe l'oeil* diagram designed to prove you can't see both at once – (it must be duck or vase, you cannot see both, but if a thing can be 'either' must it not also possibly be 'and'?) – you could see both vase and duck;

and put your finger on the one throb whose thousand repetitions make the continuous vibration of the drum-roll; see the wing beat up and down that multiplies (faster than we can see, let alone conceive of moving) into the one scimitar smooth swoop of the swallow, whose myriad synchronic movements produce the instant 'oh', when the perfectly meshed light streams one white, and life holds.

Tiny children's fingers can be made to untwist the thread from the silk worm grub, but at what cost (to grub, to children)? Unravel the thread and you break the web and at that point, he knew, there is nothing left to lure us. It gapes derelict in the wind. Splitting the light to see what it is truly made of you become hypnotised to the miraculous prism.

The man could not spend the whole afternoon standing in his yard. He had had his intense time of looking and thinking. He went in to make some tea. Thinking about the flower went out of his mind. He turned his attention to other things and time started up again. By trying to scrutinise it he had stopped it, as a rabbit freezes under the glare of the probing light of snake or car. He proceeded with his work.

The easy world going by outside his shuttered room – arranged, as Newton's was, with a pin-hole – got the refreshment of the flower opening above the wall.

37

Like the flight of the swallow

To weigh gas, it has to be in a vacuum.

And to find out how a swallow flies you have to immobilise it, to pinion it.

So to know time you must stop it, but then you too are stopped – life arrested, lustre gone from the eye as the fish dies, the ear dimmed. If we could catch the moment we would find nothing on our hands, for, arrested, what is a moment but a gap between two movements, a hiatus, a vacuum, the swallow's wing cut off and pinned, spread on a board for all to see its marvellous working – dead and incapable of moving?

Passing time

Though in a day the hour matters –

if between nine and ten say, you get through to the office to prevent the uncircumspect decision being sent out, stop the cheque, catch the secretary before he leaves for the meeting

get your application into the post, reserve your seat, get through to the engineers before they leave for their day's appointments, the order clerk before the parts department closes for the weekend (when the phone will be ringing and ringing, echoing for three days in the deserted warehouse) it will make all the difference to the days ahead as they flip like a pack of cards rippling over against each other

if you get the tractor mended in time to take advantage of the one fair week of a rainy hay harvest, go back straight away for the lost glove, the dropped tool, the omitted instruction –

yet this is of no account in the disc of the universe wheeling from aeon to aeon

so to put the collar here or there
so to bring a smile and let the hand rest safe
so the inch here or there to make the fit good
the yea or nay to set the engine going
the behaviour of the molecule in the sphere too small to be visible

indeed all our ponderings, potherings and deliberations, our concerned actions and our skilful doings
all our cleaving through the matter of existence
all our holding of breath for the papers to be brought from the conference room, the hammer to drop, the signal given
is of little consequence except in its own field of force.

And we could save ourselves the trouble, reminding ourselves, that, as the Stoics said, the only Good is Good,

except that we happen to be in this world where time operates, where the hours interlock and one card falling against another knocks them all down.

For the woodworm the only way through the block of wood is to eat its route out, passing the substance through its body;
so our way to absorb time is to work our way through the hours furnishing them with activities, necessities, goals and achievements, little piles that we leave behind, as the worm wood dust, to give us space to move forward into

collars to straighten
smiles to encourage
engine to adjust and get going, movements of funds, organisation of provisions

all the busy matter of the world going up and down and round, finding its place.

Time is money they say

If he won the prize of £1,000 he could
pay his bills with it so that when his salary went into his bank at
the end of the month it could stay there;
or since the bills got paid somehow in the end he could save it
and next year they might go to France, or decorate the sitting-room.
He would like to give a party; take his family out and not take
a bag with a picnic in it but go in somewhere and sit down and
have a proper meal.
He could send a fiver twenty Sundays in succession to the good
cause persuasively pleaded for on the radio and still have £100 for
each member of the family including himself.
So he at once became a tycoon handing out largesse, a tramp
eking out his windfall to last a lifetime of cups of tea, a recluse
with the finest cassette library, a discerning diner with whom
waiters conspired, telling him the secrets of the evening's menu, a
man whose wife and child had the latest, who went to auctions
and bought carpets his visitors exclaimed at and a man who paid
household bills by return of post, a man who changed into a vel-
vet jacket and clean shirt and frequently brought some special
cheese or fruit or flowers for his wife when he came home from
the office.

He didn't win the prize but he did get an unexpected tax rebate
of £360 and a bonus at work, together with another sum of £12
for interest calculated on some amount that should have been paid
the previous year; and an aunt of his wife's died and left them an
escritoire. It was pretty, and a better piece of furniture than any-
thing they'd ever had but Claire realised that the money would be
far more useful as it was a worry in their overcrowded living room
to keep such a fine piece from getting spoiled. Neither of them
led the sort of life that included sitting writing at such a desk – it
was the kitchen table usually with the children reaching across to
'draw my name' on whatever letter or document they might be
attending to. So they sold it at an auction and it fetched £800.
They paid the commission, the carriage, and gave something to a
charity for donkeys the aunt had favoured and put the rest in the
bank where it gradually got used up in increased phone bills and
electricity and some very good shoes for the children.

She came up the steps in the late sunshine of seven o'clock summer evening. Her parents and brother had left at lunch time for a weekend away. Everyone had been sorry for her having to stay because she was minute secretary for a committee that was meeting tomorrow morning. She wasn't sorry. She came home eagerly. Now with the day behind her what she could do with the house to herself! She'd miss the Saturday morning bustle in town and the shops would be shut and friends gone on Saturday afternoon pursuits by the time her weekend really started, but never mind, plenty of uncharted time ahead. She could eat when she liked or not bother. (The chairman usually had very nice refreshments sent in for the committee so that was Saturday lunch seen to.) There would be no worry about her parents worrying if she didn't come in at the time she'd said she'd be home. Long warm evenings, whole day Sunday.

She washed her blouse for tomorrow, polished shoes and, her room cleaned, put her clothes ready on a chair. In the peaceful expectancy of her ordered room she had settled to rubbing up her collection of glass and wooden animals, with a record on she could best enjoy when she knew there was no one in the house trying not to mind the din, when the phone rang. Oh how just right. She could say come round and have supper; or, if it was a surprise and someone inviting her to a party (Keith had got her number, she knew, but she had tried ever so hard not to think about that) she could say yes, she could come, she had the weekend ahead – they could have a party in her house, she could bring people back, they – her hoard of time was there winking and ready and the jigsaw of activities to use the hours was beginning to fall into place; and the phone was ringing.

It was the chairman of the Playing Fields Association. 'I'm so sorry, my dear, that this is so very last minute. I did try to get you earlier, as soon as I knew, but you'd left the office and obviously not yet reached home. I'm so relieved to have got you now. I thought you might be out for the night.' The meeting had had to be cancelled – the secretary's wife was in hospital. There'd been an accident. She assured Mr Bolger that he hadn't messed up her weekend and managed to say how sorry she was about the accident, and please say to Mr Smith how sorry she was. She was, but now she had Saturday morning as well.

Her suit and new blouse looked somehow silly on the back of the chair put out to wear tomorrow too soon. She put it away. The light was going from that side of the house and she didn't feel like going on with the fiddly job of polishing and replacing her glass animals. She had too many really. She rang her friend Sally but she'd gone out and her Mum thought she was busy tomorrow night, but why not ring in the morning, she'd tell Sally Shura had rung. She couldn't very well ring Keith and invite him to a party until she'd made sure the others could come. She wished her Mum hadn't left everything quite so done to 'save you spending your time on housework'. The kitchen was spotless, all the pans washed and drying on the rack, food ready in containers to save her cooking, a diagonal strip of newspapers from door to door across the washed floor.

Well, she'd go into the town tomorrow morning even though the meeting was cancelled, so she might as well wash her hair as she'd intended to do. While she was drying and combing it she didn't know why but she found that a story her grandfather had told her when she was small had come into her head. She hadn't realised she'd even remembered it. It was unlike the other stories he used to spin out night after night when he came up to kiss them goodnight. It concerned a rather nasty girl with pigtails and had been somehow disappointing:

There was once a little girl and she was given three wishes and she spent a long time wondering what she would choose. Everything she thought of wasn't quite important enough to spend one of her precious wishes on so she saved them for something really big.

Now there was a boy in her class at school who used to tease her and pull her pig-tails and call them 'piggy-tail' which annoyed her and one day coming home from school he jumped out at her and said 'Boo! Piggy-tail' and pulled a face at her. 'Oh I wish you wouldn't do that,' she said and burst into tears. Whereupon he stopped, but she had used up one wish in a temper.

The next day the boy followed her home making rude remarks and she tried to ignore him but as she got to her gate she felt something hit the back of her good new coat. She had been brought up not to throw stones or shout back so all she could do was to mutter in imitation of her elder sister 'I wish you'd stop pestering me, you nasty little oaf.' So he went away.

That night she was sad thinking how she'd wasted two of her wishes. She thought how silly she'd been to bother with the boy. 'I wish I hadn't wasted my wishes' she said to herself as she got ready for bed. The fairy who'd given her the three wishes heard her and appeared. 'That's it,' she said, 'you've had your wishes.'

She shook herself out of the reverie she tended to fall into when she dried her hair and as she went to shut the windows and lock up for the night saw there was a tiny sliver of a moon in a sky still as light as pale sugar almonds round the outlines of the roofs opposite. It looked as if it would be another fine hot day tomorrow. She could go swimming or anything.

Tracking

The two tracks on the top of the hill started as one road, the narrow grassy path up on the bank alongside being drier perhaps when the flinty track was mucky in bad weather. Then the higher path looped round over the brow and disappeared and we, making for the town, continued down the track that led to the road.

On waking everything was present in my mind together – the life of my dream, what I was engaged in yesterday that fed it, all the intentions for today, these memories not curtained by present thoughts. The channel to the senses that the palpitating day with all its effects was feeding was not clogged by the night's release from consciousness or overlaid by night images.

So all would be possible, all would be used, the aspect from the top of the bank and the tunnel of the sunken track, its stones, hard core in soft earth and beech mast.

But starting on any one of the joyous activities and tasks assumed led away from the crest where you could see how all the land lay.

We never did go back on another occasion, as, in deciding our route we'd said we could. Had we done so I expect the sheep track by then would have been grown over, petering out in minor runnels as the paths on these hills, starting so definitely and being so visible because of the light soil, tend to do.

Pocket of air

'I suppose that's what life is,' she said. 'Air. A little space where there's air to breathe, a pocket between the slabs of rock where, by some means, the pressure of the mass is held off.'

He wasn't going to tell her more of the news, the reports that were coming in from the earthquake. The Red Crescent rescuers interviewed by their correspondents were relaying gruesome details, the searching through the rubble, relatives scrabbling with bare hands at tons of concrete, old emaciated arms trying to shift wedged iron girders in case, after six days, there might be a whisper, someone still surviving in a little space, in a pocket of air. He didn't want her depressed and sickened with concern just when they had this perfect two days to themselves. He'd have enough of everyone's worry and guilt when he got back to the office.

'A little space,' he said, 'that's how it was described long ago,' so he made his favourite quotation from what he referred to as 'early literature', about life being like the bird that flew into the lighted space of the hall and, bewildered, out into the dark again.

'How lovely,' she said. Happy and full of life she could not think desolately. 'As if to say that the dark was where the bird felt safest, that he escaped the light and noise of feasting to his own safety again.'

They laughed.

He would not try and explain, he thought, or make her realise the bleakness the words really meant. 'How lovely you are,' he said, in this space of air, our hollow behind the curtain of the waterfall, enough for now.

'Mm,' they murmured, 'lovely', words being just words, without omen, to those who in the midst do not see the edge, the rock wall crushing out the space, the air obliterated by the descending curtain, for they are in life where they can breathe.

Timing

He lit the taper and went slowly to the rocket, the last best only one left.

'Light it, light it.'

'Whoosh!'

'Go on, light it,' his son's friends screamed as he paused.

He was popular with his children's friends. Tom, nine today, wanted his father to wait but couldn't say so. He had thought of this rocket as his. He was hoping his Dad would let him light it, as he had with other things when he was little, letting him use the sharp knife to cut the cake not showing his hand too much on Tom's. 'Wait a mo,' he was hoping to hear. 'Where's Tom?'

The family made a thing of all the birthdays. Tom was the youngest. To his family his ninth birthday was saying goodbye to eight for the last time. The celebration was a special one.

By the time they got to the fireworks at the end, Tom's father was tired. His hand went towards the touch paper to be finished with this party, for the rocket to explode and for him to be able to say to the tired shrill boys, 'That's it. That's the lot. Finito.'

'Wait, Dad, please,' Tom got out at the moment the rocket rushed through the air and became a golden willow tree, coins of gold rapidly emptying down the curved branches on to the earth and as quickly vanished, as snowflakes do that turn to rain and invisibility as they touch the ground.

FROM *The Rambler* XIV

5 May 1750. S. JOHNSON

...A man proposes his schemes of life in a state of abstraction and disengagement, exempt from the enticements of hope, the solicitations of affection, the importunities of appetite, or the depressions of fear; and is in the same state with him that teaches upon land the art of navigation, to whom the sea is always smooth, and the wind always prosperous.

The mathematicians are well acquainted with the difference between pure science, which has to do only with ideas, and the application of its laws to the use of life, in which they are constrained to submit to the imperfection of matter and the influence of accidents. Thus...the speculatist is only in danger of erroneous reasoning, but the man involved in life has his own passions and those of others to encounter...

We are, therefore, not to wonder that most fail, amidst tumult and snares, and danger, in the observance of those precepts which they lay down in solitude, safety and tranquillity...It is the condition of our present state to see more than we can attain; the exactest vigilance and caution can never maintain a single day of unmingled innocence, much less can the utmost efforts of incorporated mind reach the summits of speculative virtue.

It is, however, necessary for the idea of perfection to be proposed, that we may have some object to which our endeavours are to be directed; and he that is most deficient in the duties of life, makes some atonement for his faults, if he warns others against his own failings, and hinders, by the salubrity of his admonitions, the contagion of his example.

Nothing is more unjust, however common, than to charge with hypocrisy him who expresses zeal for those virtues which he neglects to practise; since he may be sincerely convinced of the advantages of conquering his passions without having yet obtained the victory, as a man may be confident of the advantages of a voyage or journey, without having courage or industry to undertake it, and may honestly recommend to others those attempts which he neglects himself.

Piece of wood

You catch sight of a piece of wood between waves as the light catches the curve of water it settles down over; it lifts with the heave of the water moving on, then slides back into its trough again where it settles to its own purposes. Balancing and swinging, accommodating to the wrappings of water, it nudges, sways down through the layers going its own thwart direction, sideways balancing till it is far away across the limitless coruscations of the sea that are the waves coming on their unchanging frontal path towards

as a key, covered in the folds of cravats, piles of sheets, the dips and folds of cloth, spaces in stuff – balls of wool, lining, bales of rugs, stacks of sloping yielding supporting surfaces – slips down, works across, now wrapped and trapped with the lifting of the pile, now on the move again, settling, travelling

our intentions slip through our days.

Visit

Cuckoo, I hear you. And an answer from across the valley.

Cuckoo, where are you? Nearer and nearer the sound. Hidden you obligingly go on calling. The child sure of not being found in hide and seek dares to shout rashly, 'Here I am, here I am.' Beech, sycamore, great trees filling the arch over the road with delicate green of a wet May. 'Cuckoo, cuckoo.' You are somewhere near.

A poplar at the edge of the trees lining the wall twinkles against the sky, ivy ombraging a distance up its height. Cuckoo, you are here; not ahead of me but above. I walk on, listen back. Yes I have passed you. It must be in the poplar but nowhere is a bird to be seen. I stand, my face horizontal until my neck cricks and I am dizzy, drinking in the light splashing down on me from the moving leaves, the gorgeous May air, the sound of the cuckoo. I straighten, walk on. The slightly mocking echo calls after me 'Cuckoo. Cuckoo.' Next time, cuckoo, I will see you.

I walk on and now the sound of the cuckoo is the distant one across the valley, echo bouncing among other sounds from the wood, part of a seen view, not the air I breathe.

I have longed to feel you in my arms to hold you, to bury my hot face in your neck under your hair. In my bed at night I held out my arms; curved them round you when your wraith crept in where I had made a space for you. I clung to you and loved you, bemusing myself into sleep with figments, figments of the body not of the imagination. I lay long in the morning willing a sight of you by my desire to see you.

When I met you at the station your neatly-fitting powder-blue shoes with stockings of a tone of grey that made your beautiful legs and the fitting shoes one stretch, overcame me. Your just-right-length skirt swayed in place as you walked smartly towards me. Of course I felt proud that it was me this enviable woman was coming to, but, surrounded by people and the day, for whom partly this scene was assembled (by the need to take on, as you had, a public life – find a taxi, a place to eat – you were hungry, I anxious), the presence that was so strong when I was alone, lamentably alone with my desire for you, faded, backed away, went down the track with the departing train into the vague unknown again. And the real person standing here really you my dream at last, more of a stranger. (It would have been insolence to run my hand up that calf, up that smooth stocking and my rough skin would have snagged the perfect surface.) The parts of my body and its movements, so right and pleasing for you in my waking dream, became ridiculous stumbling about in daylight. Oh what tussocks we have to stumble over in the lengthy meadow, boggy patches circumnavigate where the path looked clear, bramble of thorn hedges of obstacles in the hours ahead, before we can stand under the overhang of the edge of the wood far across the valley from where now, and not in the tree I stand beneath, the cuckoo sends his hidden luring call: 'Here I am. Here I am. Cuckoo. Cuckoo.'

Cork and feather

You throw a cork or feather on to the water and watch it, for its position will show you the state of the tide, the set of the current; you watch it for a reaction; it matters that it's still within sight; it is an indication of information of utmost interest. You feel if some-one called you urgently from the esplanade, even if there was an emergency you would have to stay until you had found out whether the cork would bob behind that bit of projecting rock and bounce its way into the next pool, or come to shore in your one, whether the feather would get waterlogged in the next rocking of the water or whether it would swing up and down on the surface for a bit longer. On what the next position of these closely watched objects will be seems to depend what you will do next, what the next patch of your life will hold.

Nothing very definite; the cork popples, the feather wavers. They stay in the same position while the waters go on underneath them. You realise they are gradually being taken further out. The tide must have been on the turn. There is a greater expanse of water to examine between you and them. There are other indications to watch.

Now you hear the voices calling from higher up the beach and realise they must have been doing so for some time. You move the sweep of your gaze over the whole beach. You gather up your clothes, take down the canvas strip you put up as a wind shelter for the children, make sure your keys have not dropped from your trouser pocket, watch a dog jumping after a ball in and out of the lines of foam racing up the beach far out where there are no rocks. You look at the whole panorama of the beach, the front, groups of children playing, dots of red for minute bathing trunks, or sunhats, or balls, as if to fix the afternoon in your mind and just before you turn to tramp up through the sand dunes to where the others are waiting you remember to look at the sea, now a thin line of shine far off at the horizon across light-silvered wet sands, and you remember, with a shock at your own flightiness, your inconstancy, how interested you were in every tremor of the feather, how every balancing and uprighting of the cork mattered, involved your fate in it. You look for the feather, for the cork. Never mind, it is in proportion now with all the other interesting flotsam, absorbed into the past of the day that is passing. Then you see the crumpled gritty edge, ragged, not smooth and shapely, of a feather held, drowned in the sand; in a rock pool on the clean surface where air meets water is a blob that might be a discarded cork washed up forever in the backwater it never got out of. Strange that you should have watched these tatty uninteresting objects with anxious minuteness. How much more now the focus of interest, of attention, is the wide beach, the sandy path up the cliff through coarse plants, the shore road you are about to walk along.

She met him at a trade fair, the sort of thing that used to be called an Agricultural Show held in some farmer's field with a marquee for tea and speeches and pony events for children. The shiny tractors were the official reason which paid for the hire of the two fields (one for parking cars). The presence of the beer tent validated the local newspaper's description: 'County's main social focus of Farmer's Year.' The children liked the machinery and the ponies and their fathers if needed by family or friends could be found in the beer tent where they drank with apparent relish beer more expensive and tepid than they would have tolerated without grumbling in their local pub. The farmer was always profusely thanked for allowing the intrusion of cars and hubbub on to his bit of the countryside, and saw to it that the area marketing manager of the machinery firm who was in charge of the sponsorship account (or advertising overheads against tax as it was then thought of) always had a very good time with the committee in the special members' tent and did not mingle too much with the crowd in the beer tent to be entertained by any neighbouring son of the soil prepared to harvest this annual crop from two fields useless these days for wheat, for a lower rate of hire than Danby wanted to let his 'prime agricultural land' go at. The local brewers were also profusely thanked for letting themselves be persuaded yet again to provide so much in the way of social goodwill.

She was trying to get into journalism ('our industrial correspondent'). He had come out of the army with some engineering experience and was trying to make a business setting up a technical advice service to offer small firms who were trying to break into the market for lightweight garden machinery.

If she could sell some advertising space in the 'free newspaper' she did occasional office work for she might persuade the printer who put the sheet together to let her do a 'feature'. She wouldn't get paid for it but it would be a cutting with her name on it and might get her into functions where organisers wanted free publicity. On this occasion if she hadn't known the man looking after the car park and come in that way she would have had to pay at the gate. The machinery men had their own glossy hand-outs in impeccable trade journal English all expertly printed somewhere in Germany. She could be of no interest to them. Perhaps she should learn languages and get a job abroad. One of the men, amused at a girl being interested in machinery – she would have been interested in anything to show she was a professional – did show her a new baler for want of any other audience, but switched off as a farmer friend approached bearing two pints of beer.

So she and the solitary 'consultant' kept each other company and listened to each other's ideas and sales talk. He bought her a drink and a sandwich in the tent, and she sketched out her notion for a series of articles she would do for the 'enterprise' edition the local paper ran in the gap between the 'Back to School' and the 'Holiday Suggestions' pull-out, and his truly enterprising attempt would feature in it. He was touched by her enthusiasm and inter-

51

est and managed to conceal what he never tried to from his wife – his lack of any belief in his ability to make a go of business in this neck of the woods; and she was grateful for a well-informed good-mannered man's acknowledgement of her efforts. They agreed they were both in the same boat battling with a whole lot of stick-in-the-muds, and planned to further each other's concerns if they could.

She got an office job that gave her a day a week's 'training' at a college near a town where he could drum up some visits to the few remaining light-engineering works. The area had once been the heart of the trade. So they met for lunch, the nearest either got to a business lunch, about once a month on a Thursday at a rather barn-like road house whose small red taffeta wall lights exacerbated rather than disguised the lack of cosiness, but where it was warm and the toilets clean and the chicken in the basket she always had was well-cooked and agreeably served. She did some typing for him on the college machines and read the trade journals he lent her and discussed lay-outs, and he was grateful for her conversation and her encouragement. It was the most successful point in their day for each of them on the days they met.

When the training opening on the local paper she had been waiting to apply for came up, it went to the son of one of the sub-editors – a boy who had left school without taking any exams – so his father could keep an eye on him, but the course she was doing to put her in line for that job wasn't in the end wasted. Apart from memories of companionable lunches she got talking at the college to someone whose brother and sister-in-law were looking for someone who would work part-time, unsocial hours, helping to set up an estate agency. They had accommodation above the shop, a small baby, a spare room.

The ex-army man's attempt at being a business entrepreneur came to an end when the last of the three 'family firms' he was getting work from was bought up by a brewer whose major activity was property dealing – or land development as they preferred to describe it. The site involved was a choice one by the railway 'unexploited' since the 1880s although of course providing trade, activity, work, community, life for many people through all those years as well as to the owners now bankrupt.

About this time a cousin of his wife's came to stay for the weekend with them. The teacher training college where she was secretary had a few bursaries for mature students. Would he consider training to be a teacher? Very few entrants had sufficient qualifications or interest in teaching science, mathematics or engineering. She was sure he'd make a very good teacher. She had always found him very good at explaining things. Houses at present were much cheaper in the North and they had been thinking of moving to a smaller house hadn't they?

Man and crane

As she waited on the corner she fixed her sight high above the blocks that were building across the busy thoroughfare. She hated waiting here on the kerbside. She was sure she was noticeable although it was dark these winter days a good hour before six o'clock. If he was so concerned to keep his association with her unknown, how could he not have thought that using the van with his firm's name on it and picking someone up from the street would have drawn attention, and even more so the way he drove that van. She would have much rather been sitting somewhere comfortably in a pub and he come in and they go out naturally together, her man for that moment they crossed the floor together and out the saloon bar door.

There were so many small vans like his that builders used coming round the roundabout in the evening rush hour. Every now and then she would walk along to the next corner to escape the stares and the lights that she felt all over the surface of her skin and to walk off some of the tension of anxiety that was knotting up her insides but she knew that if she were not there at the instant he rounded that corner he wouldn't wait so she hurried back. To suggest a reason for her standing there and to force her eyes to have a respite from peering at the oncoming traffic (she would count ten before she would look again) she got into the habit of watching the building going up opposite with great attention and interest.

The cranes were beautiful even in daylight. One rose quite distinct and separate like a very long giraffe's neck from the tiers of the scaffolding and grey plastic sheeting. The street-lamps' beams seemed to move like a current of water on the greasy-looking surface, though of course it was the sheeting that, even on still nights, was rippling slightly, partly hidden, from where she was standing, by the trees and road furniture on the avenue. As winter drew on the men continued working by floodlight. On the occasions when the two cranes visible above the trees and facades swung in unison, the cab of the smaller coming to rest half-way up the spire, as she thought of it, she released her breath as if she had relaxed into a smile. They swayed together, stopped, bounced once or twice and were still. 'Ah,' she thought. The two tallest cranes always had red lights winking from the extremity of their arms even when they were out of action and everyone had gone home and nothing could be seen of the delicate tracery of their criss-cross construction except when the masthead light flashed.

If he wasn't there by 6.30 she knew she might as well go, but weeks of effort had gone into making this opportunity to be available for him, so she hung on till 7 though if he had come then it would only be for her to say to him she had to go now. (Half an hour to get there at 6, half an hour to get her back bustling into the kitchen at 7.30.) Usually the van swung round the corner about ten past six, he leant over to open the door with his foot still on the accelerator, she'd jump in as it moved off and they'd go by back streets to the house she was 'keeping an eye on' once a week for friends who were away.

Even when she had the whole hour the most he was ever there with her was fifteen minutes, impatient if she even picked up the letters from the mat as they went up to the small bare bed in the back room, dismissive of any suggestion that she might make tea afterwards or that they should go round the corner to have a drink before going their separate ways. Once he was so drunk he just came off against her, clutching and grinding at her half across the seat into the back of the van, like a dog she'd seen once gripping at a child who had gone to pat its curly coat, pumping and panting on its hind legs against a lamp-post.

It was all within a period of six weeks at the nadir of the year. The crane reached, seemed to stretch to its furthest extension, swing to put the final touch on this aspiration of a building. In days the three years' hoardings were down, the uniformed doorman was directing arrivals at the hotel to the car park below the Japanese flower arrangements. The builders had vanished the week before.

It was a boring lump of a building now it was finished. Going that way on an errand in another season, not recognising where she was, she thought she'd got the wrong bus. It was a tedious part of the town. The skyline was all filled in, finished. She couldn't have remembered the make and number of his van even if it had occurred to her to want to.

Expectation

The angles of a wheelbarrow's handles invite our grasp and forward motion
as the curve of the banisters in the hall says 'Come up, come up' to where the chair on the landing holds out its arms.

And if we pause on the way up at the window at the bend of the stairs to look out it is not the garden below that we see but a distant prospect, part of a road picked out by a far beam of light on it, reaching across the town. These uncompleted lines that draw us, it is their gestures of expectation not ours that propel us, we who are led on, astray sometimes, by a patch of light on a road, handles to close our palms and fingers round, stairs that run up to an airy peaceful storey, the dip in the bed that pulls us into it.

Letter from abroad

My room is at the back of the house often in shadow with a balcony and I get a good view right across to the land that slopes up at the other side of the valley.

(For there is a road with the sun on it that I can see with two people coming down it in heavy coats and hats with ear flaps, as if there was a person who comes down the road, as if a person wears the same self [when the weather is the same], as if I am going up the road as if you will greet me and put a hand on my shoulder, arm round my back and turn me to walk along with you as if I was, as, if there was, we might; providing grounds, a road, a way to walk along, to make a road, to make a life, as if that's what it is.)

It is a great relief to get to it from the glare outside although in winter it would be dark and gloomy. I sit in the window or on the balcony when the sun is still strong on the side of the mountain.

There is a strange effect of the light on what must be a rift of pale rock because at times in half-light – as the sunlight is withdrawn up and up, as if the dusk in the valley is a solid piston-head moving up to displace the light, or like water getting higher and higher up the side of a basin, as if the great tent-like skirt of light was being evenly, rapidly rolled up from the hem until it lifts off the ridge and all that is left is a thin edge of brightness round the outline, black against the primrose clarity of the sky – you would swear there was a broad road, a white track, clear, near, accessible.

(I had presumed it was the road and had seen two people coming down it, coming to the town in the valley in the evening, until I was told otherwise. I thought if you do manage to visit we would go up there, I will explore and get to know the track in readiness so we would not waste the day, but apparently it is a trick of the light, and the hat with ear flaps I have gone into the shop to discuss buying, feeling the quality, estimating the size to fit my friend as if I knew the size, as if I bought you clothes, as if I knew, as if you were. The hat of course is not bought, I have not even bought one for myself as if for your visit.)

It is only for a short while that one sees it as a road that people might walk down, arm in arm in bulky coats, relaxed and pleasantly tired coming down to rest together after a day's exertions, exploring together. The angle of light alters slightly each day as the year moves on and once you know that the line is in fact an inlay of paler rock on a sheer surface, and the people but altering bulky shadows sprung from boulders as the light shifts, there is no road, no way up from the valley that way, no connection from the peopled valley, the life of people in the valley.

But what has come of it, what remains when the light has gone, when I know it is a trick, is a reason to write a letter, even if never sent. Mademoiselle has letters to write, stamps to buy, shopping errands to do, *choses à faire*, a life to tend that gives a point to the balcony, to sitting on the balcony thinking of one near, dear to (far from) her; point to the taking of the room so that she can have someone to write 'I have taken a room with a balcony' to; someone to whom to describe a road with the sun on it with the impression of two companions cheerily coming down from the snows arm in arm in bulky coats.

'Now in some lights,' she writes to her sister, 'I cannot get that strange formation I referred to out of my mind and have got used to the image, half from the edge of a dream I had, half an optical illusion of a road with sun on it and two short stocky people, one each side of a cart with faggots of wood piled in it, restraining it against the steep gradient with heavy coats and ear flaps (for the nights are cold up there). And I rather think in my dream it merged into the white road and the boy being taken across the border hidden in a hay cart in that book we used to have – *The Black Riders*, was it? by Violet Needham. Do you remember that marvellous book? I wonder what I'd think of it if I read it now? –'

as if there was a person expected on that road, as if I'm going up the road and a hand, the reassuring hand of the one I have a message for, falls on my shoulder and turns me round to walk along as if I was, as, if there was, we might, proving grounds, a road, a way to walk along to make a life, as if that's what it is, to write a letter, to have a letter to write, a person to write to. As if you have to go away to be able to write home: 'I have taken a room, with a balcony. I wish you could be here to see the view, you would find such a lot of interest here but I will have to make do with my limited powers of description.'

Beached boats

Even a single negative includes a positive. If I say you are not here that answer holds in it the possibility that you are indeed somewhere; moreover, might have been here, might come to get a message since someone has thought to ask for you here. Lamenting an absence means we have a friend to miss

as the sight of a clear sky includes the memory of invisible planes – oh look look, as the brilliant ribbon shoots across the sky breaking up into puffs, roseate in a sun that no longer reaches our ground, our streets. The pufflets from the track drift, reshape, becoming the cloud the sky cleared from earlier when we looked to see what the day was going to be like;

as the beached boat's frozen arc of wood, inert, holds in its stillness all the ripples of the summer tides slap-lapping against the bows as they turn the water of the bay aside,

moving through, moving out; the keel shearing through the heaving pile of water.

You make me feel cold going out in this wind without a hat

Does the curtain really keep out some of the cold, or is it the look of that shiny black bare rectangle, that gap in the protective wall that is so draughty? The coverlet of snow looks colder than a carpet of daisies. In the bleak room with no fire, dirty blankets in bundles on an unmade bed, and a light-bulb swinging on a wire high up, it was seeing the naked limbs of a doll on the hard lino that made the woman feel the cold. Had it been covered snugly in knitted bootees, lacy wool dress and matinee jacket as a baby's vulnerable body should be, as her five year old's blue and orange hands should have been covered on the way to school, and had there been some covering of hair on its paint-pocked head to keep the chill off the bone, the sight of it would not have made her feel so helplessly frozen.

If Joe came in before the shops shut perhaps they could go and get a paraffin stove if she provided the money. Meanwhile she must make it look warmer for when the children came in. There was a lampshade somewhere in one of their boxes to start with. How much shabbier things looked packed up than in use. She rolled a blanket up and spread the other as if over a couch. At least the cold-looking metal was out of sight. She tucked the doll behind the roll so only its face showed as in a doll's cot. She put the boxes to one side under a table. The room began to look more like the sort of room where people might sit round a fire, talking, coming in to warm, taking a child on a knee, as if there was a fire and warm drinks and company and fond adults to welcome and refresh.

A face with fierce bushy eyebrows and a dark hollow nostril will frighten a child however gentle and clean the person. Is the sense of touch also dominated by appearances, surface that acts as a blind to prevent physical reality getting through? In haptotica (the discussion of the phenomena attending the sense of touch) a good deal of psycho-physics comes in as if in this of all the senses most surely certain, most physical (do we not say 'in touch with reality'? Johnson felt the stone with his foot to refute Berkeley), there is most chance for illusion – an illusion of the skin and muscles, membranes, joints and tendons, a haptic illusion, play, a game of touch.

Categories of 'as if'

'There are,' he said 'categories of "as if" that we know to be so.'

['If you knew,' she thought. 'Do you know that you have a life as if you're someone else, in my bed as if you were my lover?']

'Language is the most obvious one. We make sounds as if the sound was the thing: "table", "chair"; as if they initiated action: "get me some meat", "go away".'

['Yes, you think in terms of commanding,' she thought irrelevantly, irrelevantly to her own feelings even, defensively bristling to the idea of command, like her friends, although in this instance what she would most have liked would have been to be commanded. 'If there are questions shall I say that when he says "table" I don't see a table but the pale ridges of his palate? No, a red herring, for after all I know what he means. I'm not here to show I'm clever or interestingly honest. The reason I'm here is because I want to know him, be one of the people he knows, be part of his life. But I must behave as if I'm here for the right reason. I suppose me being aware of being underhand is "an 'as if' situation I know to be so". And indeed I'm taking his lesson more to heart than the others here who know about philosophy and logic, I am acting out his teaching and that is true learning is it not? My mind is wandering (wander – can the mind wander as if it were a person – but we think of it as a person, the core, the personality, what remains when the presence is gone, the flesh has been dust for years yet the person's mind – oh concentrate, keep the grass-hopper still, for after all he is worth listening to; that you can get from him and not the other.' She came to as if from faraway although hers was one of the faces he knew to be listening, attending.]

'By referring to a presence by a word – Jean, say – we create a person before us for long enough to discuss that person. By saying, "Jean isn't here today," or even asking, "Why isn't Jean here today?" I speak as if she exists, as if she is here in a sense. Or I might say something like, "Jean is a nice girl". Now this implies a further condition of "as if". I say words as if the other person understands me, as if Jean is recognisable to them as to me, as if my idea of "nice" is the same as theirs.'

['Hardly,' she thought, 'knowing what the others think of Jean and that the reason you say that is because we always want to mention or hear mention of the beloved, as if indeed moving the name around our mouths is like bringing her here, the mind caressing as if hands were laid on frail shoulders. But anyway, I like Jean too. In that we are alike.']

'In fact if we use speech at all we assume an extraordinary range of attitudes, knowledge, agreement, and even if it's not true that both members of a conversation mean or understand the same thing by the same sound, language wouldn't work unless we could behave as if they did.

'There is then the obvious extension of writing. It is a further step along the road of assumptions. We treat the marks on paper, we make marks ourselves, as if they are the same as the sounds we make which are the same as the things and actions we want to call up.'

['Hold on,' she thought, her mind – whatever that was – engaged. 'I don't think so. I think you've left something out. You are smoothing over with logic something with more differences in than a straight continuation of a comparison. Writing is not to speech as speech is to the world of things and actions because...' but she had lost the nugget of something that made her think she was thinking clearly. 'After a bit the marks on the paper become...' but the spark snuffed out and she had not the experience of the apparatus with which to tie the thought down to let it make its point. 'To know something,' she thought, 'you have to know other things to know them by. Or rather to describe what you know you have to be able to know something else to describe it by. Just a feeling that you know isn't knowledge.']

'Now art,' he was saying, 'in all its forms, not just representational art, operates in an "as if" situation if you think about it.' Then he told the old useful anecdote about the man who stood up in the gallery at a performance of *Othello* and shot Iago and the fact that we laugh a little bit at that means we are surprised that everybody doesn't know it isn't really Iago but only an actor behaving as if he were. [And she thought of the gypsy children and women who had been in a cinema one wet fruit-picking day long ago in Worcestershire when there was no work because of the rain. They had really joined in the action on the screen as if real men and women were having a fight in front of them and she thought, 'He really is stimulating. He stirs up my mind and makes me think (or behave as if I were thinking,' she thought, 'and might not the result (the emerging thought) be the same, and therefore if a thing can only be defined by its effect would that not then mean that thinking, and behaving as if one were thinking, was the same?)' But there was something not quite normal in a person who shot an actor playing Iago. It was forgetting reality.]

61

'In literature,' he was saying [she really must listen, had she missed the link that would make the argument clear and portable?], 'it is as if it is happening, as if there is someone called Troilus, as if they are thinking, as if we know what they think (positing "as if we can know what people think" and so on).

'And history, for us to accept the role of the historian, for us to believe there is such a thing, we have to behave as if things happen.' ['Well, come off it, they do.' She re-established confidence in her own common sense. People had been killed in wars. That had happened. Cities had been built – St Paul's, and the *Queen Mary* that used to be at Poole and wasn't there any more and – people were doing things all the while. The awful thing about people, she sometimes thought, was that they couldn't help doing things. Look at the Americans spreading into Cambodia – that happened, didn't it? Certainly things seemed to happen whether you did anything about it or not. There was this uncontrollable chain reaction like chemical mixtures setting each other off, and that was her idea of history. It was true that some people were very good at behaving as if things hadn't happened – her mother went on behaving as if they all still lived in the house in Shropshire, as if Bo-Bo hadn't died and Daddy left. Behaving as if things hadn't happened when they had was stupid and led to the inexorable continuation of the chain of reactions. She could see that perhaps that was how people survived individually, living as if the situation was so and so because they would only manage if it were so, but it made a lot of problems for society. Perhaps he was going to cover all that sort of thing with a category of "as if not". But of course that would support his point and not detract from it.]

['*Wie es egentlich war,*' her neighbour on the bench muttered emphatically, meaning to be heard. 'Pardon?' she asked. 'Von Ranke,' the girl said. 'Otto von Ranke. It's all in his – ' 'Oh,' she said. Well, she supposed that all lecturers got what they said from other people. It was in the laying before you and making it clear and interesting that his skill lay.]

The rest of the lecture was filling out the categories of "as if" with examples from art and history and she listened only distantly and stopped listening to her own thoughts. She had exhausted her attention. 'Why, I'd be no good at all,' she thought, 'at thinking coherently which is what he'd expect. I'm like a person who thinks they're a runner and is much more full of go than the others at the starting point, waving to the crowd and grinning at friends, who stops dazed with breathlessness after the first lap and the others plod on and are the real runners. I have spent all my energy on being excited at the thought of thinking, and I don't really want to think at all and I'm tired and want some lunch.' And she didn't let herself get embroiled, as if by chance, with the crowd that left the hall round him, for his attraction had been that he might think well of her. She felt now that he would not. She had behaved meretriciously, claiming merit when all she could do was behave as if she was interested. Thank goodness she hadn't carried out her silly intentions of getting engaged in conversation with him. He would have known what she was doing. In the fresh air she felt how ridiculous it was of her to be behaving as if she existed for him at all, as if there were a bond, as if because what someone said struck a chord they must know also that you were alive, as if because you felt the accord so strongly they would respond to your response.

FROM *The Rambler* XX
26 May 1750. S. JOHNSON

...Affectation is to be always distinguished from hypocrisy... Hypocrisy is the necessary burthen of villainy, affectation part of the chosen trappings of folly; the one completes the villain, the other only finishes a fop. Contempt is the proper punishment of affectation, and detestation the just consequence of hypocrisy.

With the hypocrite it is not at present my intention to expostulate; though even he might be taught the excellence of virtue, by the necessity of seeming to be virtuous...

Saturday treat

A piece of fruit cake she would have. She hovered over the tray with gâteaux and the tray of fancies.

Well, fruit cake anyway, that was easy. She always had that, and let me see...

Tom came for her every Saturday from work which on that day he finished at twelve and they went to the football. On the way he bought them pie and mash at a place that sold eels. She nearly always had the same, what he had, meat pie. She enjoyed going down the road with everyone streaming towards the ground. There were usually enough people they knew to wave or shout out to. You wouldn't hardly notice it on other days if you didn't know there was a football ground at the end of it.

It would be easier just to buy more of the fruit cake. She knew Tom did like that but with all those other things it was a pity not to try something different.

After the match they came back to her room and had the tea she had got ready earlier.

The other cakes might be more expensive than she thought. She knew the price of the fruit cake.

Saturday mornings were pleasant with the feeling that the rest of the day was taken care of. In the evening they went to the cinema and afterwards for a drink at the Feathers. They liked to be on their way home before the fish shop shut so they could buy chips to eat with the cups of milky coffee she always made when they got in. They would put on records and Tom stayed about an hour and a half. She usually bought a new record when she got her pay on Friday.

The creamy ones looked very inviting but they upset her stomach. The once or twice she'd given in to their surface attraction she had been a bit disappointed. They didn't taste of much and left you still wanting. 'Is it real cream?' she asked the girl behind the counter who gazed out of the window with the cake tongues raised waiting for her decision. Whichever the girl said would be her excuse for saying no. 'What's in those little pies?' 'They're crumble tarts. Apple or cherry. They're nice.' 'I'll have two of those. Two cherry.'

She hadn't bought a new record this week. She'd gone with Lesley in the office to a disco last night. Up West. They'd spent quite a lot getting there and back. She wished Tom liked dancing and would take her Up West.

The tops of the fruit pies were all crusted with sugar with a dark red ooze where they joined the rim which was hard-baked. Something to get your teeth into but juicy and refreshing to the taste. 'Oh but I'll still have the fruit cake,' she said. 'You've got to let yourself go sometimes, haven't you?'

'She'll go back to two lots of fruit cake next week I expect,' the girl who had served her said to the other one, who was new and diligently wiping down trays. 'She always does. You see. I don't know why she has to take so long choosing the same thing.'

She chose two cakes as if for lovers.

Meeting for lunch

He'd said he'd go to Grundy's for lunch (funny name for a health food shop, he'd said). He'd get off at 12.30 to fit in with her bus to the town. They'd have at least forty-five minutes and it would be less crowded before one o'clock. Then she'd have the afternoon for shopping.

When the clock hand got to ten to one he could no longer keep his mind off the bitter thought he'd been trying to avoid since 12.35: that he needn't have put so much effort in to readjusting the working day and the fifty minutes' break of four hard-working people to rush to spend what should have been a golden half-hour, squashed at a round table that was meant to be sociable but was too small for that, in a semi-basement four steps down from a shop smelling of musty grain, awkwardly keeping a place for no one.

He decided to eat at least so that when she did come they would have time to talk and he focussed on the pictures and ornaments to keep down his increasing restlessness. Above the serving hatch there was a framed message – Victorian no doubt – lettered perhaps by a careful child.

Hitherto	(in red)
hath the LORD	(in black)
helped us	(in red).

He would repeat it five times with different emphasis and then Bratvels would appear like an actor on cue and he would show his patience and forbearance and soothe her down and not blame her and make her laugh at the way he intoned the inscription.

Hitherto   Hither*to*   Hitherto
hath the LORD   hath the LORD   hath the *LORD*
helped us   helped us   helped us

Hitherto   Hitherto
hath the LORD   hath the LORD
helped us   helped *us*

By this time he'd finished his pudding, which he enjoyed, and decided he could go now. No face, wisps of damp chestnut hair sticking to wide forehead and cheeks flushed from anxious hurry had appeared searching for his at the top of the steps: Bratvels – messy, honest, full of concern, clumsy and very dear to him. No rush of apology for him. Immediately to forgive and reassure. His firm strides away from the café smote the pavement to the beat of: 'Hither*to* hath the LORD helped *us*. Hence*forth*, I'll be blowed if I'll wait.'

The sky at night

It was one of those blustery nights when, if you look up, it seems as if the stars are being blown about. Hither and thither they swing because the cloud wrack is racing high up in the sky but you don't see it as moving cover on this night of no moon.

She got up, went upstairs to fetch something, came down with something different in her hand, started to rake the boiler in the scullery, went into the sitting-room for the dustpan, leaving the boiler door open, and to get yesterday's newspaper. She started tidying a stack of magazines she'd knocked over, forgot the newspaper. Should she ring him? Yes, why not, do a thing when you feel like it. She went to look the number up and found herself walking away from the phone. Later, when she had a cup of tea by her, on the table where the telephone and its notebook and pencil sat with just space for the tile, later she might phone. That could do with a wash. The blue and green bird gleamed when the tea stains and dust were washed off the glaze. She smelt heat – the boiler door, Lord! Flaring away. She was getting as careless as Joan. Come to think of it, you did take on the habits of the people you lived with, out of self-defence perhaps. Perhaps she would write instead. The ash next. She became engrossed in the sheet of yesterday's paper she had in her hand. She must have picked it up after all. Tomorrow; she would leave it till tomorrow. She must concentrate on what she was doing. She would not write of anything serious until she knew he wanted to be interested. She felt so light-hearted. What a pity she could not see him now, when she would be light, almost flighty. She could tell him – oh all sorts of gay things.

Roll on the day when he could have his own phone and not have to always be getting change for the pay-phone in the hall. He hadn't been going to go out but it was a nice night and a little blow wouldn't hurt. Tom and Mackie might be in the Cross Arms, the nearest place to get change at this time. He could even phone from there. He'd be back in time to record the programme. He could do the veg then.

As he was changing his shirt there was an arresting clarinet run – ah, must just listen to this.

Must've left his keys in the bathroom, changing. No, they weren't there. What had he been doing? Bathroom, tapes... Looking through his drawer to find an empty tape for when he got back, he took out six others. I'll listen to those and sort them so I know what's where if Elizabeth does come round. 'Come and listen to my tapes.' 'Come and see my etchings.' Oh no, that was not what his tapes were for. He couldn't really listen if she were there, perhaps preferring to talk and being polite about jazz. Better take her for a drink. There his keys were, on top of the radio. But time had slipped by and if he went out now he would not be back in time for the programme. When it finished he dashed down to the Cross Arms to get the last fifteen minutes of pub time. Tom and Mackie had gone by then, but he became involved in the explanation of the pub's name that the landlord, who prided himself on his interest in local history and quirky bits of information about origins of phrases, was giving a visiting American. 'That so?' the chap, clean shaven in a jacket and tie, was courteously saying. 'That so?' tactful enough not to supply the landlord with the more accurate knowledge that John felt sure he was in possession of. He bought the American a drink. Most people cadged off Americans, taking advantage of the feeling Americans were often encouraged to entertain that as they were richer they should pay. He had spent six months in Chicago. He liked America, he said. Couldn't stand the wind and the feeling there wasn't a hill or a wood or a valley in a thousand miles or anywhere to walk to, but loved the architecture. To be able to make a carpark a beautiful building visitable as a cathedral – ah, if only we could copy what's good in America. The car has ruined our cities.

As they strolled down the road with assurances and hopes of meeting again 'Fine night,' the American said. They looked up. The clouds were racing across the sky. Occasionally a twinkle of light flashed out and then disappeared. 'What did you say you were in?' 'Peas,' John answered. 'Agriculture?' 'No, engineering research. Canning. It looks as if the stars were moving not us.' 'Why surely you can take more'n a coupla pints before you start seeing stars?' 'No, I mean the clouds dashing across make the stars look all flung about.' 'That's another thing we don't get in Illinois – your wonderful skyscapes on account of your changeful weather.'

When he got back to the house it would have been far too late to ring, even if he'd remembered to keep change for the phone. He got out a report on algae pollution in Lake Erie he'd kept but never really read and decided he'd better eat something. He could ring her from work tomorrow if he felt like it.

Fly

How many times have you watched a fly against a window-pane? Again and again it goes on to get into the light that surrounds it but which it is somehow being denied. That is so obviously the way out. Persistence will bring it there in the end.

But of course in each direction it comes not to fresh air but to a barrier. The way up is the way down so off it sets again, or hitting an object down it falls to manfully pick itself up and start again.

You offer it your finger and would free it, will take it round the barrier through the open gap at the top of the window. The fly thinks you are the worse danger taking it away from its one chance, you are now what it flees, you are preventing it achieving its escape, for see here is the light and that way safety and life lie which it would have reached had you not risen up, a panic danger, just when it was going to get through. It flings off back into the dark room and then hits again against hard glass with frantic buzzing again.

And do they, you wonder, as you finally manage to scoop it with a newspaper up and out through the window, do they think once they breathe in unconfined air and slow down from their desperate struggle, that they have escaped the dreadful situation by their own skill, that even that last and worst hurdle of danger they managed to surmount; that they are saved only by their persistent adherence to what they knew, passing along somehow to other flies their lessons learnt from experience of how to survive this particular danger, that the hand which in fact effected their freedom was the menace which they, with luck, with struggle, strength, valour, were escaping from?

And should we learn from this that sometimes the very thing we are fighting is what is helping us to survive (the uses of tribulation etc)?

And as wide of the mark as the fly (if it does think that) is our putting human reactions on to flies. Situations may be parallel. The details of one may illuminate another. But it is far more likely that we are comparable at base to them in our actions, our processes, than they to us. For they, together with the tides, the fluctuations of the year, the composition of the soil, the formation of the rocks, were there before we were, we being a late and curious sport. How could the fly think of motions out there as being the result of some benevolence coming to its aid when that idea is a little side-line, an extravagance we have thought up, we with time to dream? We do not figure in a fly's life as they do in ours. It must be all the same to them whether a morsel of stickiness is to be sucked up from a mound of pink flesh which may be the soft underside of a baby's arm that brushed the jampot as it stretched across the table, or a natural flower supplying its food in the order of things.

The fly has got in again. It is once more buzzing frantically on the pane. Once more it refuses to realise that the shadow following it, the paper closing up on it is its very aid in time of trouble and not a bird going to snap it up.

Once more we think: 'stupid fly'. All that we, and the fly, can imagine is from the little circle of what we know. Our idea of God can never be God's idea but only made from our capacities, and therefore no God. To the fly we will never be anything than what we are to the fly. And even that is our idea.

Here we go again.

The fly starts again to crawl across the surface of the glass.

Honey in February

Look, a bee on the door-handle. In February. How on earth did it find its way so unseasonably into the kitchen? In fact it was trying to get a grip on the yellow brass handle on the outside of the door but the glass made the reflection appear inside.

The unaccustomed warmth must have brought it from its doze before the aubrietia was out. Perhaps it had expected shiny celandines and was drawn by the glint of the metal, metal warmed by this splash of sunlight in a sheltered spot doubled by the glass of the pane in the door.

Surrounded with the excitation of company, the hubbub of other people's buzz and busyness, the warmth and glow of hospitality – wine in glasses tipped, straightened, raised, winked over to indicate: here we are on the inside, here a dropping of guard is appropriate, necessary – your face glowed, open to interest, open to approach, bright-eyed.

As it tried to secure a firm position to lower its proboscis for nectar the bee's feet slipped on the hard edge of the handle. It clung, ungainly. It was marooned. Showers would soon sluice down.

And as uncircumspectly my thoughts winged to the sunshiny flower of your mind in the spring, the false spring of the year.

Flight of steps

As the sack of the body goes plonk plonk down the flight of steps into the dark the metal edge of each step is firm and hard under foot, as if rising up to meet it, hold it, almost slap the ball, bear upwards. Drop drop drop loose from the hip you can let the body go with minimum exertion until you firm up when step pushes against foot its own weight, rather than a step down taking it down, because step after step will be there, come up against it, solid, firm, rigid, upholding. Next. Next. Next. Drop sustained using gravity only, no lifting of legs, because of these sure supports. Down on to a step. It holds you before the next tilt forward, next fall, next leaning on the strength of the hard flat step.

Would you so sustain so support weight that the mind of another could go according to its natural fall, in its élan, relying on your firm hold, your level platform to land on, without a stagger, a crumpling, a twisting with the weight on the wrong foot? Would you sustain so, just by being there, the being in its natural fall into pull of gravity?

Would you so sustain me?

Categories of 'as if' *(cont.)*

'Still considering "as if" situations,' he started the following week, 'we move on to the area of moral actions.

'We set standards of behaviour "as if they were possible". For instance, we tell children, "You mustn't lie; nice people don't hit each other; it's wrong to steal." We make these statements as if the world was like that, as if we lived in a society where people don't lie, hit each other or steal. In relation to goals and intentions, the child might be asked, "What are you going to do when you grow up?" as if the child will have any power over that, as if a person of whom one asks that can know what life will be like. There is a difference between what people say and what they know, what they say and what they do, for in order to have any control over the circumstances of their own lives they must at least convince themselves that things are as they say. Even a determinist like Hobbes carried on as if human beings had free will. To decide something, you have to behave as if you believe you can decide. People behave, for example in spoken assumptions to the child, as if certain tenets – being honest, loving your neighbour as yourself, owning up, not saving your own bacon at the price of another's – are what guide their own lives although they may very well know that "real life" is different. Quite obviously this sort of statement-making is used so that people have power over others – priests, politicians, teachers, yes, even lecturers [disarming smile – arrogant world-weary cynic, thought Liz's friend], office chiefs, employers, anyone in a position to claim to know more than the advisee. For instance, people make quite different assertions implying knowledge to a foreigner or stranger seeking information than when among their own compatriots.

'But it has another use as the glue, if you like, of society...'

[The rain started sluicing down, making the hall darker and colder than before. He knew he'd lost their attention even while trying to make the theories they needed to know about alive to them in the actual experience of their lives. They couldn't be bothered with that. They just wanted safe notes on what Hooker said, what Hobbes represented, the Lockian world-view. He missed the eager open face whose attention had kept his interest going in what he was saying last week. He would much rather strike off suggestions in a small seminar where the students could fill in the examples and details for themselves, but here he had doggedly to go through the points which the diligent could take down as if they were copying a text book. Extraordinary how even now whether he found what he was saying convincing depended on whether his listeners were impressed and held. The same lecture could be good or tawdry accordingly. Perhaps if he spoke as if that kindly admiring face were there fixing his, impressed, he would get some interest back into his voice and then he would sound good to these dough-nuts. Or did her absence mean that she didn't think it worth com-ing again after last time?

It was all so obvious. Students usually were more interested in moral questions than aesthetics because they felt it applied to their own interests, they were all interested in behaviour, and prepared to talk endlessly about their own and others', but they did not think that the 17th and 18th-century ideas on morality and education that he was about to refer to were at all interesting or relevant. The girl with the sunshiny face and crinkly dusty yellow hair would have been interested – or polite enough to go on listening. And it was interesting. And she would have got something out of it. For the point of these quite wildly impractical ideals set before the child by the holders of wisdom of the tribe was to keep society going. You could not tell a child of five the truth about the world or they'd give up there and then. Someone must put it about that the ideals were the expected norm, so that before the light of experience made pragmatists of us all, a few anxious souls would go on striving to make it true.]

'As a man with very exacting standards of truth-telling in his own life said: "With the hypocrite it is not at present my intention to expostulate, though even he might be taught the excellency of virtue by the necessity of seeming to be virtuous." ' [Would they get that connection? With their wailing self-righteousness about "sincerity" they would dismiss Johnson as a pompous hypocrite, and wasn't he a Tory and didn't he take a pension – how the lack of compassion of these young puritans made them so boring] 'and to Johnson, if anything led to virtue it was to be encouraged. An "as if" situation if ever there was one.'

[What did they care about the agonies of conscience of people who believed they were sinful? They were all probably much more like Hobbes, without of course having read him. Probably.

He was getting too far out on his limb. He must come back and behave as if he wanted to charm them, like last week. They must go away feeling they had learned something, take away a portable little packet with a label on. If he was in Clair's room, now, talking about the merits of hypocrisy to him – well, he must try and talk to these dispirited youths as if he were with Clair.]

'We are used to associating the dualistic attitude with Descartes' division of reality into two substances – thought and extension, that is, the world of objects out there provable on the senses and the intuition within, which allowed Descartes to abandon his step by step method and make a great illogical leap and presume the existence of God. But the roots of this division really go back to philosophers in an earlier age who also tried to reconcile their quest for scientific truth in relation to a world becoming more measurable, with their deeply embedded beliefs in mysteries beyond human comprehension.

'Now, where Hobbes's particular reconciliation comes in...' [He had got their attention again. After all, Hobbes was on their list. He continued fluently, usefully, absorbed in his material and it was only at the end when he was packing up to go and the students were drifting out that he noticed the crinkly dusty yellow head of hair at the back. She had come then. It was as if by behaving as if she was there, he had made her appear. She had come, he thought, at the point when the lecture came to life. Sympathetic magic. Virtue rewarded 'by the necessity of seeming to be...']

Suspension

1. When the rain stopped the plastic-covered twine strung across for the washing held drops twinkling in the clearing air all along the line like a curtain rail with hooks hanging.

2. Late afternoon the occupant of the top flat practised. In the summer when the windows were wide open she heard him practising runs; over and over he did a trill which ran up to high C which he held, held, held, longer and longer each time

3. The child was given an apple by the greengrocer who fancied his mother. She let him hold it but told him to wait till they got home to eat it. He looked at the greeny brown curve flecked with yellow orange and his teeth itched and were dripping with spit as he imagined biting into that full curve, that was the best bit, the first bite

4. The door into the garden stood open and a low shaft of sun was painting a band of flawed ruby on the rises of the three bottom steps of the stairs that led up from inside the back door

5. Waiting for the removal men to return for the last chests which were already on the pavement, he jumped when the phone rang vibrating the bare boards of the top landing

6. The dog stood in the middle of the path immobile except for the quivering on its lifted tail and its palpitating nostrils, one paw lifted

7. The dancer was on her knees, her trunk circling circling quicker quicker wider wider her hair a curtain that followed her head

8. The child was told to go and say goodbye, they were going, and stood face lifted at the bottom of two long legs that went upwards

1. Two flighty birds chasing each other landed on the line swaying back and forth and as they pushed off, the line discharged its pendants.

2. just within the point where he would burst, she thought, and just when she thought she would burst, he cut off the note.

3. until he found his tongue against the cool roughish skin his top teeth stuck into the convex and the juice pouring over them and dribbling down his chin.

4. the stairwell filling with dusk, when the breeze that came with evening caught the door and slammed it shut.

5. because it was so loud and, the house having been emptied of all their things, he didn't realise it was their phone, that they were still connected. By the time he'd got upstairs it had stopped and silence filled the air as completely as the wild ringing had done.

6. then was off in a beige flash, to the bushes on the right.

7. and just before he thought she would surely split in two, and his back break with the tension of watching it, it swept her up into a spiral and in one swing she was running round the edge of the stage in a wide circle, hair hands and tunic streaming behind her like a flying bird.

8. and up into a round belly and up to a white shirt when came a red face at the top with large black gaps that widened with moist yellow teeth and moist dark-veined linings sprouting wiry hairs

which, bending down to kiss him, became his loving, loved Grandpop.

Sphere

The golden image is the perfect round.

The bubble caught the light becoming solider therefrom, solider with iridescence; but whole, but airy. Unbroken. Complete.

The egg is smooth and whole.

The Greeks particularly thought the sphere to be the image of perfection. No edges. Nothing further to do. Rest.

Words are spiky with edges trailing. There is more to come and a tangled mass behind. When he started to speak, to tell, what he had meant got distorted, it became different. The image came out a squashed thing as a ball in a distorting glass looks pulled sideways like plastic material – rubber or plasticine or malleable dough or the stuff they mould into shapes with round edges like art deco furniture, and then it sets and is brittle – not firm and clear with a curve to fit the palm, like glass, like stone.

The beautiful small globe, catching the light as it drifted, disappeared. The explosion was not noticed but there was a drip or two of suds on a leaf.

The porphyry smooth curve of the egg is chipped and gashed by the chicken getting out.

The stone is incorruptible. It is finished. It is whole. It will not grow.

Silence keeps the image in an indestructive atmosphere, as specimens are kept in sterile bottles. The image thus preserved will not rot but without words that change, recharge, disturb it, it will fade, as bottled fruit will not rot but lose colour and taste if kept away too long from the affecting air.

Cake uncut

The cake uncut
Soil cleared, the earth turned and left unplanted
The bed made, the counterpane drawn smooth;
Radiators drained, tools cleaned, oiled and put away
The table cleared and polished, the new book on it unopened;

A new pad of paper, unmarked, the letter not yet written
The telephone fits well in its holder, not ringing,
The convex of the apple is uninterrupted. There is no jagged
    browning indentation from a bite taken
The curve of the cheek is unkissed, an unmarked nectarine

The bud of the flower.

Party

The knife cut through the icing, spilling out currants and crumbs,
    and an embarrassed mother wondered why the birthday child
    was grizzling. 'Too much party, I suppose,' she whispered
    ingratiatingly to the calm mother of a well-mannered guest.

The evening darkened, bringing in the horizon, closing flowers
and windows. The road leading up round the flank of the hill
seemed to end where the brow met the sky.
    It was still visible if you knew it was there, but where it went
into the shadow from the hill, it seemed to be cut off like a con-
crete strip in the middle of a field not going anywhere. Because
of the lie of the land, once you were on the road you couldn't
see where it was going as you thought you could from across the
valley.

The child cut into the cake that for three days before the Birthday had been enthroned in the larder, its silver ruff an aura of expectancy and invitation. It was a long-premeditated and longed-for action as if the hand were a fish drawn by the lure of that smooth surface through a time-track of three days. When the knife went in, and the hard shells of the beading were crunched and there was a messy edge there was little point in the party going on, for the Birthday was over. They might as well all go home. It was not the meanness and greed for which the child was reprimanded that had upset it when the cake was split up and shared. The cake had been The Birthday Cake. Embarked on, it was no longer there to be wondered at.

It had disintegrated, vanished, as a white track becomes obliterated by the dusk that eats up the light.

'...and sun and wind like love...'

If the face of someone who we want to love us clouds over we cannot move, we go cold.

The smile of love is like sun upon the face, and I have elsewhere described the sun as like love upon the face. But if I said this to someone who lived in a country where there had been no rain since they were five?

I always wondered whether the saying in *King Lear* was a misprint, a bit where the text had got garbled. You know, where Kent is in the stocks and, thinking of his master's disgrace, says, 'Good King, that must approve the common saw Thou out of heaven's benediction com'st to the warm sun.' Surely heaven's benediction was to be in the warm sun, not avoiding it? For me the warm sun was a comforting thing not the enemy, and surely in an Elizabethan winter one felt the misery of cold even more than now, so how could being warm enough mean losing Heaven's benediction? The sun is our blessing. So I had to think it was a hot fly-ey day when Kent was put in the stocks, with no shade, like the days of picnics we used to go on when the grit got under your sandal strap and your legs rubbed sore with sweaty heat; when it had been a 'glorious day' and all you longed for was to be home, with cool water, or at least in some shady spot, and not to have the five miles space through the open bright meadows to get across, which had seemed so enticing and never-to-be-tired-of in the morning.

So we have to go on saying what things are like; not that things change, not that the sun and love and happiness in a child's face and the lightening up of its face and our longing to be liked have not always been the same, but that there are so many facets to things, to the words we use to reflect them there are so many reflections, refractions, so many paths to them, so that each time we must nudge the little wheel, if ever so slightly, for the focus shifts in a turning world and the hand on the minutely adjustable wheel of the microscope, while our eye is glued to the lens, vibrates if ever so slightly, and we must keep adjusting our glass, we must angle the beam. If we stop the truth becomes dead, dead not as a stone which is incorruptible and is before truth, but dead as a bone which was for another purpose, there for all to see apparently preserved in the earth we turn up to lay it out to expose it to view, to reveal it, but light and useless as a dead bone.

Love letter

How can I describe the sun to you? It is like a barley sugar, like a barley sugar when it is sucked translucent and is full of orange light like the sun.

As the poet says: 'Love is a climate, is a way of light.' The train surges over the bridge above the river. The wave of sound and the rhythm is like the water waves pounding on the beach, the long line of the oncoming water perpetually moving its weight onward.

How can I tell you how I love you?

When another train came the other way the sound was not the same. I tried to think what it was like this time but could not find something to describe it with. But because I had thought of the sea's thrash and withdrawal and return the earlier rhythm of the other train came back into it. I shall have to wait for something to strike me from impressions again around me, to get it right.

I realise I am acting on the assumption that if I can get it right, that is convey to you very precisely what it is like for me to be here, thinking these things, you will know how I love you. If I could make you understand one thing, you would at once know the other.

But then I also realise that this is not so at all, contrary in fact. Because my longing for you has materialised you – so near and so far – does not mean you are thinking of me, although the you I have brought before me is there only by thinking of me.

I am among the crowd drifting along the esplanade by the river. Perhaps you are concentrating at the moment on something else I know nothing of, or dispersed among many others. This and this and this person whose face, whose form comes across my view – for me to register their outline, their type, for them to be real even for the short time they are around me, I have to make them, fix a shape on them and it is based not on them but on something in my mind.

In an embrasure at the foot of the bridge, a corner made by railings above the river, a man picks up a flute. He has curly matted hair and the face of the roguish tinker on the cover of a book from childhood. Lean refined features, high cheek bones, a twinkle in his eyes, a sweet mouth, gallant gestures, neckerchief. I stop and listen and stand there listening and looking. As I go slowly on over the bridge the sound of him playing is still with me. Other sounds come from the wide river, the view expands, impressions from the extended world flow up. Part way I stop and look back, face back detecting the small bit among a mass of pieces, the man whom I would not have noticed or heard from here had I not seen him separate and close earlier. Face towards the people coming up over the bridge from that side, one woman caught my look as she passed. She reminded me of you but this made you seem further, more limited because it was not you. Why could it not be you? While I could still see the musician it seemed I could hear him. From out the crowd, across the air, the to-ings and fro-ings cutting across, the wide aspect of the river at that point, the areas the train track cut through curving south, London pouring around, I felt he knew I was there, that something of his playing was directed at me, that while I looked to where he was he would be aware of me across the indiscriminate crowd. An older man, he was, using his charm, responsive to response. He would have recognised the state I was in, appreciated my appreciation. I strained to pick out the sound of his pipe as I went on over the bridge further and

A train thundered across and all was banged out and when the air was clear and transmitting again the sound had gone.

I lost the thread, the man, the scene, the crowd, me in it thinking. All was left there, finished for me and I walked away from the river into the town. You are far, you are tiny because the place where I thought of you, confined you to talk to you, has ceased. I am tired and spent. Perhaps whether or no I can tell you how I love you does not matter to you. If you were here I would not need to think of how to tell you. I would not need to tell you. I would not have to make you up from out of the flux of a crowd, the rhythms of a train reverberating over a bridge, the surge of the sea, the charm of an actor drawing money to his cap with his smile (playing for money after all), another woman who was not you.

Diver

Naturally when we meet to talk you ask me how am I, what have I been doing, what seen? as, naturally, that's what I've come to tell you –

Waking we come up through layers of sleep, as divers do who wait to break the surface, breathe the air, fill their lungs with the waking world again –

to breathe the air, and tell you all that was held with the breath, all that was down there, in the depths.

I turn, moving in wide circles, moving slowly, coming to, in the air and as I emerge the rope sinks backwards beneath the surface, uncoiling gravitationally into invisibility, in a mirror movement to my rising up to greet you as in the day one might catch a glance of something, a blue pullover lying at an angle

and think, was that in my dream then, that the child gave it me, or is the recognition of the shape of the elbow of the left arm where it is worn a glimpse from the shifting past, obscured at once by the swirling particles of mud that the groping stick stirs up – something buoyant being released through the surface up into the air that makes it visible, to sink at once into the next suck of the current, fathoms down out of reach, out of sight, out of the day,

leaving me with no cable, no support, little choice but to shut the door behind me and go out into the light of day, with not so much as a good story to tell of where I've been, what done, to you who kindly ask how am I?

Dazzle of the clock

She looked up from the lightless street she was going along to where the church clock was visible in a gap above the roofs. The sun had struck at that height from across the frosty valley, a shaft from the clear wide morning sky although it hadn't reached the pavement, and the clock face was all a dazzle of bright flashes having been recently re-gilded so she could not tell the time and could not look long on the palpitating shafts of light shooting from it,

as when crossing the road I was suddenly looking into your face unencountered for so long except in my thoughts, always in my thoughts, and could see nothing, and could do nothing; and each continued on our way, the time not told,

and remembered an occasion driving to see friends in the dark countryside and coming into dense fog at a roundabout, and creeping round and round, hugging to the right, not able to leave, feeling rather than seeing – the more you looked the less you could see and strange shapes began sawing up and down in the air above – unable to launch out over to the left – quite sightless to find any turn off and the opportunity once passed not available again – or a way back, and suddenly as if the windscreen had shattered, the lights of a car behind hitting the wing mirror right by my eye, sending up dazzle through the eye to blind the brain and no way out of the danger but to go on, not to stop, somehow to leave the round-about and get away from that paralysing shaft

as one has to move somewhere from the stunning explosion of love.

'The Sun in Splendour'

From living with three days of hauntings, rememberings, imaginings, I came to meet you in the pub – in the snug you said you'd be – through the fog, encased by the dark of those days that never opened up all day just before Christmas, to the cigar-fragrant pub which had battened down its hatches for its favoured afternoon regulars – endless dark afternoon of a December day that had lost time, strange cut-off days through from dusk to dusk, from lighted office to the mysterious dim alleys the fog had made of known wide thoroughfares, patches of thick air lit by bedewed lamps high above us and all we could see was the top part of the lamp-post up in the air and a little circle of dark of damp on the pavement directly under it; as if we were marooned at an airport, or in an ark with the rest of the world drowned;

and you were sitting on a stool, sideways to the bar facing the door I came in at, your clean white shirt without a tie open at the neck, such a beautiful soft boy's neck which rose from between your shoulders, the muscles of which rippled under a black waist-coat stylish as a snooker player's; and although I had only seen you once before, casually at an office party you had been brought to though you didn't work in the building, you, the centre of that circle in the dark shabby pub, chipped formica-topped tables smeared with a patina of the lunch hour's stickiness and ash, no splendour even of signpost or blazing fire, brewers' sham Dickensian, you whom I only knew in waking dreams, greeted me, welcomed me, acknowledged me as if you had been waiting only for my arrival, had put all your attention to expecting me, as if we were together, as if we were together on the flaming bridge, cut off from either bank by the fires of desire roaring at either end, preventing rescue, preventing escape. And we sat drinking rum and cloves to keep the damp out of our chests, you entertaining the company, your friends, your lunch-time regulars, your colleagues, your life, it seemed to me, me drawn into the company, witty, relaxed and attractive from being considered so, from the rum, from the atmosphere, the droplets from the fog, now forgotten behind the door, still in my hair, on the collar of my coat; and warmed by what seemed your flaming silky reddish hair (but perhaps you had a light behind you for later Margaret referred to your hair as brown) and the light of excitement in your eyes and the ripple of happy desire in your skin as it moved over your limbs, for you had asked me to lunch, you were entertaining me because you had met my friend Margaret and you needed to talk about the beloved, and wanted to know your chances, and what her position was and whether...and with the intimacy and security of confidants, colluding over the campaign for love, what close old family friends we could be, sensible go-between adept at crusty practical advice, putting forward only your advancement, her attributes.

But like the sun you could not but let your beams fall on me who crossed the path of your trajectory, and so I basked in your lustre, and so I was drawn in.

You saw me to the bus stop and waited till a bus came, and I thought there were no buses but didn't say so, content to stand there with you until the weekend, till the spring, and we were surprised when suddenly one stood beside us, like a ghost bus emerged from a dark lake, and then as suddenly you were swallowed up into the white invisibility and the next day when morning came the fog was not there and it was as if there never had been any, and the place we had been in vanished from the town as if we had gone back, or to the side, in time. Everyone went back to a normal working day.

And I have never again been into the Sun in Splendour for I wish to retain that oystered pearl, never cut out, never used, to feel that I have known what it is, that feeling, that joyful flame of desire, that lit you up, pure stranger, and shone on all who came into the sphere of your beams, like the strong sun of early summer as it springs into the sky.

Cats' eyes

'Oh, but I like the adverts,' she said. She was bubbly and did the talking and you didn't have to worry too much that she would disapprove of what you said or what you liked. I had grown up in a rather critical family – lots of clever older sisters and me the only boy. My parents genuinely found a lot of the trappings of public life distasteful and intrusive and, though outwardly welcoming, rather winced sometimes at friends I brought home. I'd relaxed a lot since I'd left that careful well-endowed household where I know I was the apple of their eye and where nothing passed unnoticed but it took me a long time to lose the fear of offending – I felt people wouldn't want my company if I didn't like the same things as they did.

So I enjoyed being with Sharon. She was easy to please, and always expressed appreciation if you did any normal little act of attention, like noticing if her feet were hurting her, or helping her on with her coat and carrying things for her, and when I first took her out expressed both pleasure and surprise at what she called my generosity. I think she'd been among mean people who'd taken her for granted and since she was good-natured and strong she'd just accepted that she'd be the one to fit into other people's arrangements, fetch and carry, and pay her way, and often for them too.

'The one I liked best was the Shell one. You know, there was a petrol pump with a man's head sticking out of it, well two heads really, one looking down the road and the other in the other direction. And all it said was – there wasn't even a car, just streaks in the road – "That's Shell – That was." It was really clever. It really looked as if the man was moving his head in a flash. I wish I could draw. I used to try to move my head like that to look two ways saying, "That's Shell that was," or "That's Tracey that is"

87

(she's my older sister) till Mum got fed up and said I made her feel giddy and I'd rick my neck. And it made Tracey mad.'

Just for once I could cap her anecdote from my own experience. I didn't usually say much personal about my family for I didn't want to draw attention to the very different homes and childhoods we'd had in case it made her feel awkward or think that I was what she might have called snooty.

I was going to tell her what had come into my mind about the cat's eyes but it occurred to me that when she was a child her family might not have had a car so I said I'd spent hours trying to see exactly when the light in the fridge went off when you closed the door. I thought there was something in there playing a game turning the light on and I would snatch the door open to catch the little mannikin who puts the light on for you, off his guard, sleeping for once, perhaps, slow from eating up the cherry-pie that I knew was in there for tea. But I never caught the point where it went off and *my* mother had got annoyed because she'd been making ice-cream and I must have not shut the door properly and it all melted. (The bit about me spoiling the ice cream wasn't quite true but I was learning from Sharon to amuse people with little anecdotes about oneself and I wouldn't have wanted to show my mother up in a rather sour light by saying that she complained at any sort of noise or repetitive action that seemed to her to have no point to it and she probably thought I would wear out the mechanism.)

At that point the usherette appeared with her tray of ice cream round her neck and I was able to enjoy Sharon's reaction to me buying her an ice-cream. She always wanted me to have one too, but for myself I don't like eating in cinemas or in the street, and we settled down to making remarks about the trailers for 'forth-coming attractions', which no doubt annoyed the people around us but which we thought wildly funny. Oh Sharon, if only I was sitting next to you now (now now NOW), your firm leg warm against mine, your fingers intertwined with mine on my knee, your recently washed hair curling on to your shoulders, your whole-some warm smell, your softness, your niceness, oh how my skin longs for yours, my face aches to bury itself under that curtain of hair, my shivering body to be wrapped in your ample one.

But it was the cats' eyes that Sharon had reminded me of. You must have, as a child as I did, travelling in the back of a car, per-haps going home in the dark after a Christmas outing, looked out of the back window to try and see if the cats' eyes still shone after we'd passed. Surely they must still be there, the toy cats, in case another car came along. But turn and twist as I would in order to see the road behind at the same time as the road ahead with its jewel-like line of green lights zipping up the middle, by the time I could focus through the window on to the dark at our back we had sped on to open up another seemingly far away stretch, the lights of which in their turn were swallowed by the front bumper and wheels, to become indistinguishable from the darkness behind when it was fed out between the back wheels. Somewhere under the car those reliable green lights were extinguished.

I wanted to marry Sharon. I'd have given up my medical studies, done some job that fitted in better with her family's way of life so as not to separate her from them because I knew she needed still to be part of them, whereas I had already moved away from mine. But she wouldn't have me, or rather she said, ever so kindly, that it wouldn't work. She would have accepted me I think. We were happy together and she was far from set in her ways – quite adventurous, really, without making herself too noticeably unconventional. But her family couldn't – her brother more than the old people. (When I got a job in the factory where her brother worked, he did everything he could to make the other men hostile to me working and eating alongside them, and when the manager wanted to 'promote' me to take a job on the administrative side, saying the firm didn't want me to waste my education by doing a job that wasn't fulfilling my potential, I knew where the suggestion to move me from the bench had come from, so I went back to medicine.) So Sharon, who had more talent and spark than the rest of her family put together, conformed to their idea of what would be acceptable to them; and I suppose I have done the same.

My parents would have accepted her willingly. They were opposed to me giving up on being a doctor but they were open about people – far less snobbish than Sharon's family as it turned out – and wanted my happiness above all. They would have liked to have a daughter-in-law they could include in their love.

When I try to remember just how that well-being and happiness with Sharon came about, when and how we met and our love blossomed; and at what point and why it became for her a love that wouldn't 'work', I cannot spot it, turn and twist in my mind as I may to look back from the lives we now lead to that time, that lit-up time, increasingly obfuscated by the layers we lay down by moving through the present.

On the wing

As a bar of light goes out as you cross it, for you have dispersed the shaft by standing in its trajectory

as a cat, where no cat lives, skims across the threshold when you are not looking (you look up only to see the vestige of black flash on the air)

as the warmth, enough to blur the ice fronds on the window pane, goes when you put your hand across it, the sun blocked behind the interposition

as blobs of loose snow that, wandering through the air are caught on your hair, the fringe of your scarf, your cheeks, your nose, but on the road instantly disappear into it leaving small patches of wet blue black

so waking we try to catch the receding drift of thoughts

so, awake, we try and grasp the fancies of our imagination that, to us in the day, are as dreams when we sleep.

And maybe these untrappable phantasms are but the fumes from the bodily functions, and the hope to net them as much wishful thinking as to catch with outspread arms the shadow of flocks of birds a mile high winging and fluttering on over to another continent – thought on the wing, black flash from floaters in the eye, the air formerly charged with exhalations now cold and empty;

thoughts dispersed, the message scrambled, the line gone dead, the seed blown; the spent rocket nothing but ash and bits of charred debris in other people's front gardens and Mary Rose nowhere on the island.

Dog searching for rabbits

An elderly man was sitting on the bench above the track that crossed the hill just below its brow, so commanding a good view. Most middays he came as far as here with his dog, getting home for lunch at 1.

He loved watching the little dog ferreting about, letting his nose take him, and the old man's eyes, hither and thither down towards the valley. The old man was thinking about his father and what a clever man he'd been. None of us, he thought ruefully, inherited his charm. Trained by their mother's doggedness rather, we were, except for Helen – bright Helen who'd gone abroad and died. She had those winning ways. He remembered the phrase. He thought it had originally been his mother's. Perhaps she'd got it from a song. He hadn't thought about his family for a long while. He didn't need to. His memories of them, set long ago, were fixed furniture in his mind. But something about this still late autumn weather, and something his neighbour had said – What was it now? never mind. Something about manners.

There was still a faint sunlight where he sat and a heightened but restful light off the remaining gold, light brown, reddish leaves. It was warm with a bit of mist thickening down in the valley. 'Chip, Chip,' he called. Didn't want him lost in those brambles if fog was coming in.

Now what was that word that was so appropriate to his father – not dishonest – though years later he'd learnt that he was that. Chap, chapbook – some word that sounded like that. Crestfallen? No.

Chip must be over on the left down in the dip there – he thought he saw something moving but maybe that was from staring into the mist, a sort of optical illusion. Optics, optical, obtuse, hypocrisy – no he wasn't a hypocrite, nor yet a plain liar. Elusive? Was that it? No, he felt sure it began with a C. He tried to think of a sentence. Optic, opp-, pop, no, population, popular that was something else; tried to imagine someone who'd known his father talking about him. Character, charming. He remembered him tipping his hat when he went into shops. He was always nice to shop-girls, though he could be surly at home at times.

A white projectile hurtled out from some bushes on his right in full chase. Oh Chip was having a glorious time. 'Hey Chip,' he called, 'don't go too far.'

Calculating. That was it. Well that was what he was – very, but he was sure that wasn't the word. There was another word, something that turned things to his account, quick to see how he could – oh dear, Chip had gone further now. He knew he was down there. He could hear little yelps and see movements and shapes on the edge of the mist where it was lying down along the grass and pushing itself up the hill. Pushing? Effrontery? No, nothing like that. He did hope he wouldn't have to go down the hill over the tussocks to get his dog. He banged his stick on the bench and whistled and the sounds echoed through the still blue air round the hill, its limpid frailty carrying them far. The dog suddenly shot across the hill racing up to the man, his tongue out, floppy ears banging up and down, then all muddy paws and slobber on the man's neck and face.

Ah, got you. Expedient, that was it. That was the word I wanted. He walked sturdily home, his dog beside him. 'But I doubt if any word would really do to describe my father. I'll write it down when I get in and remember it begins with ex.'

By the afternoon the mist had rolled up from the valley and covered the hills.

Wind moving clouds

As flitter the shadows on a fitful day, making the water now dark over the dense bottom, now translucently polishing the different pebbles, yellow as sucked butterscotch

so into and out of her mind passed like exhalations, images of intentions:
'Dear A,
        I have now decided…'
'Aussie, my dear,
        I'm thinking of going to live on a farm…'
fading as soon as heard and voiced over into 'No, I shall keep off writing and see what he does. "I was thinking about writing to you," I shall say when he comes. "I decided not to." The interest wakes on his face. He would say…and then I could bring up…'

The water darkened again along the stretch of it visible from the copse on the hill.

'Cancel that conversation.' The less the better. She would not be drawn into explanation. Just a sad smile when – no, if – he called round and a 'let's enjoy the evening now you are here' would cut out pointless round and round cul-de-sac argument and it wouldn't be her to be blamed for always reducing their meetings to petty goings-over.

The light strengthened over the field, moving like a wave down the slopes to the river, brushing its bank with a faint paint of yellow.

There he would be at the door, she would open it she would be sprightly and ebullient and not downcast. At her best. As she was when she was on her own thinking of him. He would be glad to be welcomed. He had been wanting to come all the while...

but the undefined light disappeared into itself before it reached the water's edge and crept back into the ground. The field went dim and the water cold.

Arguments of 'but you should/shouldn't have; I did/didn't do; would have if you had/would have if you hadn't said you...'

Detritus-filled cul-de-sac.

She took the bucket of hot water to scrub the scullery floor.

'Dear Bernard,' (that grimed grease round the cupboard feet was coming off)

'I suddenly wondered how you were. Can you give me a reference on the Ottoman Empire? Dan is going to Turkey (lucky devil!) and wants to read up about it. I said I'd find out something for him and thought of you. Also any advice about accommodation etc and what not to do gratefully received. (Memories of *Midnight Express* – wasn't that a good film? Do you ever go to the cinema now?)'

Well that unurgent possibility could be pursued later if restlessness demanded some outlet, but she could as well go to the library and find out about the Ottoman Empire herself. Bernard would be totally surprised to be the recipient of such a flimsy pretext. If he answered with advice it would be like a serving gone cold, nothing coming from it. There was nothing there. Never had been. He'd been her brother's friend, but Dan didn't want to bother.

While she was at the floor, she could clean out that old cupboard, rusting cake tins and slightly greasy balls of saved tin foil shoved there – ages since she cooked cakes twice a week. Why not make a cake? Nothing foolish or deridable in that. She'd leave it to them. Then she'd know if they wanted to. They would if they did. Which they didn't, plainly. So what? It let her out.

The sun splashed full on to the water from the other side of the river, the clouds were moving over, the wind now forceful now still. Why couldn't it decide one way or the other? Still, better than steady definite rain perhaps

these volatile vapours scudding chasing and changing shape through her brain.

Shutter in the wind

A thud every now and then. A crash. Stillness. Then another deliberate smash, but no tinkle of anything broken. She looked in the bathroom – nothing – and closed the windows and doors of the rooms upstairs.

After yesterday's curtain of rain today's sparkle would let her go right ahead like water in the cleared channel. She was glad now that she'd swapped her day off with Julie. Yesterday, snug and dry in the office, would have been a write-off at home. Eagerly she got her things together. Dull air and backache had made yesterday unappetising. Today would be all go. The air was bright above the hedge that the kitchen window looked into, beckoning her out.

The shutter banged in the wind. The intervals of the clashing were irregular. The sound was noticed only as an indication that there was wind about.

When she got to the corner she saw the postman going up the other side. She went back to the house in case the cheque had come, in which case she could bank it and pay the electric while she was in the High Street.

Maybe the catch was not off but had worn loose so that when the wind was from this unaccustomed quarter and made a sudden buffet it soughed up and down. It seemed to have stopped now.

No post, but by now she had started looking for the electricity bill. She had better check it against the meter. She had said to Geraint, she remembered this now, that she would be more orderly with the bills. She was going to start a system, files, boxes. This was a good day to organise a system. She sat down on the stairs to check the addition of the bill. She multiplied 1142 units by 5.078 pence three different ways. Something was digging into her left buttock, surely not the stair-rod? Oh that's where the stopper to the hot-water bottle had got to. How on earth? She put it straight away in the kitchen drawer. Well, it had been worth coming back for the post then, even though there wasn't any; she wouldn't have to try and get a new stopper now.

The shutter was still. The hall seemed dark. It was very quiet but as if someone was listening, as if someone was holding their breath.

None of her figures tallied with the figures on the bill. Having the box of household bills on her knee she started to put them in chronological order, then it would be easier to compare one year with another to see whether they were really using more. If you knew how much you were spending, it was easier to stop it flowing away – literally down the drain in the case of hot water. She had satisfactory bundles for telephone, gas and electric, rates and water were smaller piles. She'd get some elastic bands so her work would not be wasted. She was considering whether she couldn't throw away the last red notice since she was just about to pay the bill when the telephone shrilled. Her knee jogged. The box spilt. Wrong number.

A sort of rustle was followed by a terrific bang. Surely this time something must have smashed – but it might have been thunder. Then there was a sigh that became a hiss of fast rain. With papers strewn on the bottom stairs and all over the hall floor, she looked out of the front door. The wet blew in her face, clammy leaves on her ankle. There was a river rushing down the gutter. She couldn't go out in this. She'd go when the storm had passed.

In the end she didn't get out till nearly one and returned dispirited half her errands undone because the offices were shut. She wandered up to the bedroom with some thought of sorting the dirty from the clean clothes, made the bed and thought a bit gloomily about Geraint and how by the time he came in, the direction would have gone out of both their days. Having the smooth surface of the bed cover available now she moved clothes on to it so she could sit in the chair and putting the clothes into neat piles made it seem as if the jobs waiting to be done on them had been. She started a letter to her sister Kathy – after all she could see to the clothes and cleaning when the children were in chattering around her. As she wrote thinking up things to say which would be warm and friendly, she found herself suggesting going to a cinema together next week, looked up the cinema in one of the papers strewn half under the bed, jotted down the times, scooped up the pile of debris and the cat with it from under the bed and got the hoover up into the room.

The wind though fitful, was becoming stronger when it blew. The banging became a rapid run of retorts, as if a hand was slapped, palm and back in $2/4$ time against a cushion or a head. When she went out again, to buy ingredients for a cake she'd decided she'd make this evening and to post the letter to her sister, she'd go out the back way and see to it. It was a bit of a task getting into their yard because the heavy side gate hung at an angle and dragged, one hinge being broken.

Yes, she'd go out now. Now the day was moving fast and she was racing time, but running with it. Oh but there was all the mess in the hall to clear up, three years' household bills that would have to be re-sorted. In every room was something unfinished – nothing was either concluded or put away. She put her hand in her pocket to check where she'd put the key and finger and thumb tested a piece of paper. Cleaners' ticket? Receipt? Cutting? Oh, the electricity bill. After all that she'd forgotten the main thing when she had gone out. But after all, it could be left till tomorrow. And the other things. They all seemed a drag. Better stay in and finish off here.

There was a great quiet in the house as she came down the stairs. The house seemed to hold its breath but not painfully, there was peace within the rain. The sound of the steady rain curtaining off other sounds showed the wind had dropped. The rain was falling straight now.

She felt smart in the grey mac and fitting ankle boots she put on. Why stop for a cloud? She would get a file in that new shop next to the post office, get to the electricity board today after all. When she got back she'd get the meal under way first. Half an hour concentrating would tidy the worst in the house. If Geraint came home soaked it would be good to have the meal ready and the kitchen cleared. She'd get the rice on first.

As she came in, determined to stop the banging that had made the day restless, she realised it was the wooden gate itself, swaying on one hinge, the top occasionally catching against a drainpipe. It made an awful noise but wasn't really doing much damage. It was slimy and her mack was new and clean.

When Geraint came in she and the two children were on the floor playing Monopoly in a sort of barricade of the chairs on which washing ironing and books were piled.

'In a muddle love?' Geraint leaned over.

'Not really,' she said, 'the lull before the storm – it's only surface – the meal's on – you do mine for me,' she said to the ten year old, 'while I make some tea.' She hugged Geraint fiercely in the kitchen. 'Oh before you take your wet things off would you stop that wretched gate from banging? It's been annoying me all day.'

The wind rose again in the night. There were thuds and bangs and rattles and wheezings from ill-fitting windows, loose garage doors, shed doors propped with bricks, unshut gates.

Geraint, sleepy, made as if to get up and go downstairs to stop the banging. 'Never mind now,' she said gently pulling him back and covering him with the bedclothes and wrapping him and them round her, 'it's next door's. I expect it'll stop soon. It's OK here.'

'I'll say,' said Geraint.

The dawn was damp and still and quiet, with a sense in the air that it would clear later, and the household slept.

Gnats

The gnats swing up and down up and down as if they have to exert pressure against the air above them to push themselves down, as if gravity is tugging them upwards. They press down only to bounce up off an invisible trampoline with occasional jerky zooms at an angle to mingle with another part of the group where they all tread the air together. Within this cloud of gnats there is a constant re-arranging of position but in spite of this movement their group is almost as defined as a plank of wood which, for all the see-sawing and dashing about of molecules, stays in the same place.

'Darling, lovely party,' the forty-five year old – whose visit to sunny lands in January had bronzed but wrinkled the skin of her cleavage, loose like a plucked goose's under the cross-over of a jersey dress – made her voice bell out in her greeting to her hostess, but her eyes looked beyond to see what faces above what shirt fronts had arrived and which she could give the opportunity of paying her court a little by bringing her a drink. Not Geoff, no, she could lunch with him in the week and he was busy being the perfect butler. Ah, there was a face, clean, lean, young (ish), doing courteous duty, no doubt, listening to that mousy girl from Natalie's office. Charming, she did appreciate nice manners in the young. She would rescue him. 'Do remind me, Natalie dear, of your little secretary's name. I must go and say hello to her and I'm afraid I never can remember that sort of girl's name. Congratulations, by the way, on Geoff landing the contract. Is this a little celebration?'

'Let's get some food, Abby, before the crush. There are one or two people I want a word with and then we'll cut along pronto, shall we? Unless you want to stay?' He left a plate of food in her hand and seeing that she would not be standing with no one to talk to as an energetic woman was making her way over, went to have his words, first with someone who occasionally had work for photographers, then with someone he'd done some crewing for last year to let him know he was still around with his health and strength and his pleasant ways and his looks.

'Abigail, how nice to see you,' the warmth and attention was in full flow before she realised that the target it was aimed at had moved off. She perforce continued affably and did in fact find herself interested in the girl and the work she was doing in Natalie's office, thus acquiring a little background as a base from which she might acquire a little more so that she could seem to be almost 'one of them' – rallyers round Geoffrey and Natalie's concerns. And Abigail Posthwaite, who had her mind in a relaxed sort of way on one of the files she would have to get to work on tomorrow (being not a secretary but a sort of peripatetic accountancy consultant on the legal side) and also on the fact that soon she and Rodney would be sitting in the quiet of a cinema, found her a pleasant and a kind woman and enjoyed talking to her.

Geoffrey was taking coats and making sure of the ice. He was relieved that Emily had not made a beeline at him. Now he saw her being such a useful guest he felt a bit mean that he'd suggested to Natalie that they didn't have to ask her every time, because she was a good sort, talking to anyone who seemed to be on their own. One thing about these theatrical types, they did like meeting and talking to strangers. With some people you wondered why they ever went to parties – there was Danny – he would stay in that corner, holding hands and talking to his latest popsie all evening, making no effort, when forcibly introduced to someone who wanted to meet him, to pretend that he found them of the slightest interest – but 'interesting' people who Geoffrey invited for other people to find it worth coming to meet only came if they thought there would be 'interesting people' there (people they thought it might one day help them to have met, to be in the circle with) and Danny, his dull and bad-mannered brother, was apparently someone worth meeting for those to whom the City was either bread and butter or golden dream. Geoffrey was glad to be able to provide. And Danny came so that under the respectable cover of a family visit he could offer a girl or two – even if it was not his hospitality he was lavishing on her – a reason for wanting his attention.

Geoffrey came to fill up Emily's glass and shepherd her over to Danny so that the popsie who was already showing she couldn't take her drink, or rather Geoffrey's, might be slowed down in her exhibition of intimacy by the presence of a social chit-chatterer, and also to make Emily, good old sort as she was, feel included in family. Emily was not one of the people for whom Danny was an attraction and soon drifted back to Natalie.

'Anything I can do to help, Natalie darling? *Lovely* dress.'

Gnats have long many-jointed antennae which is probably what enables them to jostle without colliding.

When most people seemed animatedly in conversation, heads getting closer, or, content not to be so, emboldened by the buzz and the food and drink and the activity around them to hover for only a short time before making a beeline for what they wanted to join, when, in fact, the party had "gelled", Natalie did at last drift from group to group, making sure that Geoffrey's uncle, who was something in the City, felt comfortably enough attended by nice-looking young people. She thanked Rodney and Abigail on their way out for sparing time to look in. She saw that Geoffrey was relaxed in the kitchen checking up on reserves for latecomers and making more ice, at last tucking into some salmon mousse himself and talking golf and Scotland to Freddie. She went swiftly to where a young man with a floppy lick of fine hair he brushed out of his eyes when he saw her coming, was examining and piling up cassettes by the player. 'Rodney's got me tickets for the performance on Thursday,' she said. 'Want to come?'

The gnats yo-yo up and down up and down with occasional purposive zooms but always in the same square yard of air about five feet above the ground in the lee of the dark hedge. They seem to go unwearyingly on for a long time, and, slightly mesmerised, you can stand and watch for a long time. Then suddenly they are gone. About other business? To other feeding and mating grounds? Who knows? The light that enabled you to see them against the dark hedge has gone, the path along the canal disappears, as the furnishing of a room when seen from the outside and the people in it cease to exist when the light has been switched off.

Probably they, or other gnats, will gather in the same conducive haunt some other summer dusk and we may become aware of their activity for a short while – a short while out of what seems a perpetual positioning, re-positioning, re-aligning, keeping themselves afloat.

Bagatelle

In our bagatelle board there is a gulley to project the metal balls on their circuit and you push a little stick fixed into a head the size of half-inch dowel through the covered bit the track emerges from. The ball sits neatly against the end of the tunnel. You know exactly what has sent the balls on their way, when your movement has gone smoothly into a strong stroke, when your fingers have slipped on the hardly thicker-than-a-pencil rod, stubbing the ball of your thumb or banging your knuckle knocking the board because the stick is too short. It was broken off long before we came by it. We were always rather better at adapting and making do than following instructions for games and perhaps this as much as laziness was why we never fixed a longer stick to the pusher so we could fire properly. It added the need for a skill to the elements of chance.

Some boards have a shiny button you pull out. When you let it go it shuts fiercely as it is on a spring and the balls clatter round with the same force each shot. The mechanism is hidden. To the infant watching the balls it is adventitious, like a bird singing now and at other times not, and perhaps more interesting to it because of that, although it wants to know, it wants to touch, it wants to make the balls move.

And where is the trigger for feeling so that I could tell how the mechanism worked, why one day everything is inert, averted, difficult, even picking up a spoon a heavy task, a decision to be made and fought for? There is no momentum behind what impels brain and hand to leap for the same things as when a twined rope is thrown to lasso a bollard on the quayside. For at those times the patterns and actions and responses in the brain that flower into words, speech, writing – that are as much as bone part of the fingers' business, netting knotting knitting, doing whatever at any time needs to be done – have gone dull, dead, like the sharp outline on a white wall when the sun dims. There is nothing there but uniform wall, but blank.

And another time, seemingly no more propitious, we are all go. Things seem to get done on their own, we are the needle eye through which the thread runs swiftly, actions which, yesterday, our faces closed, were left undone as mountainous tasks. The waft of the air energises as if the sun was pulling out the scent from the flowers. You lift the phone on your way to somewhere else and in ten minutes do weeks of decisive business that brings a long ripple of other steps taken in its wake, the line of water pushing it all up ahead of it like a carpet unrolling. How can you have spent so long yesterday wondering whether, thinking not, opening the drawer and shutting it again, circling and backing away? Today by the time the post has come you have got your post ready; as you answer, you file; as you change, you hang up your clothes. Thinking of pie for supper your fingers are already mixing the flour, you cleaned the bath in the same movement with which you got out and dried. It was the seven o'clock news you listened to, thus releasing the hour between eight and nine and (for it is summer) you gave the grass a quick swish with the hook before the dew had dried from it – it will be a hot day and too dry and dusty to do when you come in tonight. (Half done now, two more quick swishes, two more early mornings, have it done that way by the end of the week.) You fill the cat's dish in the garage as you hang up the hook on your way in again; or (for it is winter) seeing to the boiler and the ash away listening to the news, and while you're at it filling an extra hod in case it's wet later, so your wife too can start her day without the debris of yesterday choking her action; getting the car out (cleaning the windscreen the while and checking oil) so you can have breakfast feeling ahead, on top, in time (and away before the traffic takes and shreds your next hour to a rag, another hurdle in the obstacle race successfully jumped, all the better for the next run up the straight) on top of the hill, on top of the morning.

And why cannot it always be so easy? And truth to tell most of these things get done on the athwart days, but oh so heavy and entangled.

Just by watching the balls speed on from a good shot we cannot say that the next is going to be the same. Although it should be a matter of will there is involved also something we do not know the working of, some spring we cannot see, laws of physics which we cannot alter, only adjust to.

Making a cake

He had come quietly to stand in the doorway and watched her hands moving in and out of the dough like nimble fish tumbling, passing through water and round and through again.

He thought he had almost learnt the mechanism that set her going at full efficiency, like those cars advertised 0-60 m.p.h. in .5

of a minute, seemingly in one movement from inertia to the cake cooling on the rack. It would take him longer to decide what to make.

She was trying to move a strand of hair from off her cheek by jerking her shoulder without interrupting the working of those strong small fingers with the even pale half-moons at the base of pearl-nailed tips. He came across and cleared her face of the hair and kissed her floured eyebrow and she jumped. Uff! How long have you been there?

And the fish sank to the bottom. The rest was thinking what to do next, looking for things in the clutter on the table, clearing it, willing the result (and of course the cake got made, an outsider would have spotted no difference in the action or time taken).

'What gets you going?' he asked. 'Do you decide in the morning you'll make a cake for tea? Or do you find yourself drooling over the recipe book and get tempted by the pictures?' At that moment he was being very restrained because the image that not his eyes but the ache at the top of his thighs was producing was of his right hand pulling back the bedclothes with one movement while he held her close up against him with his left arm, his elbow pinning the small of her back and his left hand spread firm on her buttocks pressing her into him, lowering them both thus clasped so close that not the edge of the thinnest piece of paper could have got between, her rounded soft warm body sunk into the soft clean bed and him surrounded in that softness. Want, want. The words did not move his lips. He felt them groaning in his belly. There was something he'd become unjoined from that he must close up with again.

'Of course in German they have the same word for do and make: *machen*. Perhaps that's it. To make something you just do it.'

'Is that so?' she said, opening her eyes wide at him in pretence of mockery at the same time running her forefinger round the bowl and offering it to his mouth to lick. 'You mean we English sit in a slump and wait to be told before we make anything, but the Continentals just up and do it?'

My! she was quick in an offbeat illogical sort of way, his nimble silver fish.

'No,' she said, when they were in bed, 'it's not just having a picture of a cake in my mind. I might be thinking of clearing out the cupboard or something – I don't know. I just have a thought of me doing it and I've started. Sometimes perhaps I'm thinking of you.' 'So it is just sex after all.' 'No, you dirty old man, thinking of you coming in, silly, and asking what's for tea and I see you biting into a piece of cake and my teeth go all salivary and then I make it.' Nevertheless he was turning over in his mind whether volition towards these actions was not activated by the sexual urge wondering if she was going to sleep and would mind being re-awoken when, chewing his ear a bit, she said, 'If it worked that way why isn't it that when you feel – you know, like that – you don't leap up and fix the shed or clean the windows?' 'Hm,' he said, getting her small body totally covered by his long one. 'It doesn't work that way with me. I'd rather fix you. I'll do the windows tomorrow. I really will.' So they did.

Tiller hard to port

As a large boat under way in a crowded harbour will not seem to respond at first when the tiller is pushed hard over, for it takes time for the rudder to check the weight of water and pull the hull round against it

as an engine in the damps of the morning may turn over with a clatter, with whinnying, with urgency that leads to no other sound but lifelessness when you take your finger off the starter

so we may feel all our effort is getting us nowhere, heaving at something we are powerless to move, running hard on the spot, no distance covered, only our blood pounding; incompetent to change a thing, lift off the weight, further an action, get it right, get it done. It will never turn in time.

Suddenly the prow swings round, the engine fires, the stone turns evenly on its fulcrum;

and we spring off down the track.

Window

The casement window was wide open all night, the weather being so still and warm continuously through the twenty-four hours that inside the house one could not tell whether doors and windows had been left open or not.

As the dawn light brought the window frame into being the grey wall of the gable adjoining this part of the roof at right angles became visible at the back of the open pane. Thus there was a rectangle of the stone (here and there paler, here and there darker with a stone's irregular surface, some tinges of almost-yellow where lichen would be) that was glazed, and round the edge – through the wide hinge-space and in the long-sided triangle at the top – there was the direct sight of the wall, apex of roof and sky round ridge-tile. Also visible from the bed the dark metal curve of the lever-type handle against the glass, against the dawn; and as clear, as dark, as defined, the inside curve of this handle, the inverse, on the outside of the window. But there is no such handle outside the window. This solid-seeming metal object with the clearly defined edges, catching the light on its curve, whose line and definition gave such a lift, such a calm exhiliration, was a reflection. And then in the wall but the wall still there, every bit visible, there: chimney pots – dentillated pots above square stone parapet, television aerials laddering into the sky, red round ceramic pots, a single, a pair, going down a line as figures standing on steps, one above the other in stages, these chimney pots and roof edges marching into a tree top.

Move a little, the white boards of a dormer projection come clear as if emerging from the stone wall (the stone wall that is there beyond the window) yet, cut off half-way by the gutter half-way down the gable-end, the stones seem to overlay the boards.

And the real trees seen through the open window-pane, in the gap between the windows, and through the other closed half of the window, have another great bank of trees mingling in them, now in them, now clearly standing outside them as the head is moved, raised to look or sinks back to sleep again. For there are more trees above the roof gables and edges, squares and slopes, outline of windows in roofs, projections, gardens, sheds, walls, outlet pipes bending round gutters up into the air, different textures, different colours, that proceed down the terrace on the left, not visible from this window, this position on the bed over against the far wall; this window that looks south over orchards and grass to a great wall of trees in the sky and the sky beyond, and the only building in sight, this end gable of the house of the neighbour on the right, his orchard and his shed there, his grass. And in the space of sky between this sloping gable roof and the far mound of tree-hedge as the light grows, a cedar top hangs in the sky without stem, separated from the things that grow from the earth by a streak of cloud in the blue sky.

For it is a tree there but not there, its ghost-self, its perpetual mirror image. Move the head and its extreme branches now are impasted on the board that the roof tiles of the next-door house are fixed to, the strip between tile of roof and stone of wall. It has moved in the turn of a head from far out there in the sky to that wall I can almost touch. It is sky-tree or wall-tree as one moves, manoeuvres. Clear as clear either, though.

And in the window also, at the hinge, the part where the window is closest to our own house, is the other half of our window, with its edging of eyebrow, the short overhang of tiles over the dormer.

So the lives are all there at once through the window: clear air, view through glass, and much other life contained there too that physically is elsewhere, elsewhere but contained in the wall, in the window. And the one does not supplant the other but the one shines through the other, provides container, means for the other.

Now you wake, for whom the window is open or shut, a window or a wall, the life in a wall one of stone, the air something diaphanous illusions may move through but not occupied with objects that should rightfully be elsewhere, today not informed with yesterday. The window is a thing that is open or shut. Windows are for seeing through not into. We must not confuse object and reflection. This is for this; that, that. Day is for this night for that. Friday evening this Monday morning that.

'It's too early to get up. What are you doing up there? You'll catch cold, come back to bed.'

I look at the town and the trees and the sky hanging in the glass like that other life of a tree that hangs over water. What feeds our feelings and connections with each other if not this life suspended in the air, coming out of the stone, intangible, indisputable, drawing us to it, provisioning us, reflections of otherwhere, ripples into today of what we have thought of since yesterday?

I withdraw from the window. I come back to bed. The window swings shut and wall and air are separate and left and right move back to either side. Inside is inside and outside outside. The wall becomes plain wall, the life in the pane disappears.

Goodbye love.

House by the lake

What the lake has made of the house and its verge is so clear, so exact a record. The reflected buildings are the more receivable, more encompassable, more solid-seeming being presented in the element of water, whereas the reality of air shifts things, clads in ambiguity, brings affecting currents from elsewhere, making you feel, sometimes, you are in a place altered from what you had been expecting

as when we meet after absence, after a time when our meetings have been much (and only) in the mind (half-way up the stairs on the way to get something from the cupboard, going home in a crowd of people where thoughts can go free because no one knows who one is or what thinking and imagining – sweet soft conversations in our heads of what we feel for each other, expressions of love, acts of reassurance: dialogues for one);

and find each other, and ourselves with this longed-for other, to have strange unassimilable angles, aspects unknown – or not accounted for – awkward surfaces of knobbly actuality that did not hamper us when building up our thoughts, our reflections.

House by the lake II

The tree, the punt, the blades of the reeds, puffy white clouds
on blue, and the frontage of the boat-house, are so clear, are such
solid, such defined things in the liquidity of the lake

as we (70% water) seem substantial beings to each other.

Maybe the base which gives rise to appearances is what you
can't see: the seven-eighths of the iceberg, the distance down into
the earth that is required of the builder to match the upward soar
of the skyscraper, the things that happened before you set out to
meet me by the lake in the park.

What brought us back and back to this meeting place was the
extraordinary reflection. That's what caught our eye first as we
came through the gap in the hedge from the road: the clarity of
this presentation on the water as if on the skin of metal
as the flutter of your fingers above the crowd at the station was
what caught my attention, and your hand on my shoulder as we
reached each other returned my recognition like a ball zooming
back over the net, doubles bounding back from facing mirrors.
And, real or not, this is what still catches our eye, the apparent
solidification, sharp-edged ample bright buildings, with their boat-
houses, grassy paths, punts on the lake nestling into the edge, clouds
sailing in the clear blue patch in the water.
It is the brightness of people's eyes that draws our attention, the
bit that is really nothing being the most magnetic of all.

In a glass

We went into the huge building and I was glad we had come; glad too at your pleasure that we had managed to include in your visit one of our monuments.

There were innovations since I last showed someone London's symbol for awe. There was a big revolving door, no doubt to keep the temperature even inside the cathedral so the cold Easter winds should not snatch away the heat and make soar the heating bills; and make shiver the visitors and make miserable those standing in wonder looking up into the dome.

We gazed at the beautiful black and white diamond flagged floor with the small stone inset commemorating plainly the men and women of St Paul's Watch who by the grace of God saved the cathedral from destruction. St Paul's was full of people, as it was intended to be, admiring, exclaiming, going to and fro like a town on market day; looking, sitting, thinking. It was a lucky stroke that the grandeur and pleasantness of London was working and that we'd come this way.

But what I remember apart from the glow of your appreciation, what I see when I think of the occasion, what I see it through, is the special new glass of the revolving doors that in fact you can't see through; for as we came up to them they threw back the reflections of the people coming up the steps on to the portico, your eager face, the skirts of a mac swinging open, street furnishings, roof edges of buildings down Ludgate Hill. We faced the sky behind us, the outside world, then our own stretched and funny figures lurching towards the centre; and like a road which swallows a car at the horizon in a film shot, all those coming up to the edifice had their reflections pulled in, twirled round, and disgorged invisibly, for you could not see into the nave, you could not see those who had been landed on the other side, inside; only their reflections surging round as someone else pushed in.

The people were shepherded warm and shadowless within the great shell, their shadows, their reflections, their seeking images shut out and twirled away into the air outside. The irregular muffled thud of the door swinging round separated the unseen real bodies from the clear sharp outlines of what after all has no body, no being; eyes that gaze but cannot see, cannot answer others', breathing skin and lips that do not even mist the glass that holds them and that withdraw behind the brittle block of the surface at the touch of fingers on the glass.

Fog at Wotton-under-edge. Perspective

As when on a misty morning getting up in the warm dark of the sleeping house you look at what appears an unaccustomed scene, as if you had been put in the middle of a Cuyp landscape in the middle of the night, the broom handle in the half light presenting spire-tangled woods as if engraved, the strange patch of light on the floor from a street lamp not yet extinguished: a lake between dark slopes; all that full secret life going on in the house that sinks away as the full day shows reality,

so the reverse can happen and the actual features of an area we are travelling through seem embodiments by which we can delineate and bring to clarity the movings of the mind.

We are struggling through the small circle of one movement, the dinner-plate of fog, the whole world consists only of the thick air up against you, only a little pocket of air to move in before the enclosing wall that moves with you, up on the Edge, the world gone, nose and eyes pushed into present circumstances; only the present and only the space taken by the body is available, our senses ground into the here and now so that in fact we are sightless and deaf, for we only see and hear by looking before and after. Suddenly, between one second and the next, one foot's space and the next, a cut-off as sharp as a cliff, suddenly you are not in it. You see the whole valley, the line of the hill, the lie of the land, the railway line leading out, clumps of wood on spurs leading back down other valleys, houses and spirals of smoke indicating movement, activity; tops of factory roofs, cars moving down the valley road.

So, on properly waking to a day, enclosure in the obsession of loneliness, stiflement of loss, desertion, vanishes as air comes in, the false friend is but a little dot among others and is now elsewhere; and the full bustling valley spreads below with all its delightful distractions of gorse and butterflies, the track to it visible and open.

Contrapuntal: Two pears

The swell of the dark blue pear glowed into the beige of the coverlet. The twining stem of the rose without thorn outlined the declivity where his bent leg humped the bedclothes. Dark soft reds and greens flowed down – fruit flower leaf – into the dip where the eiderdown lay soothingly on his thigh, and spread up the slope the other side. The trees on the island with the birds singing – the island he'd been aiming for, for the gala, for the festivities, all through the busy day – they were going to be lit up in the evening. Weren't they? He wasn't there. They were disappearing, as a fog blows in. The details and colour were turning away, leaving obscured shapes. Then there was nothing. He was still just near enough the reach of the borders of sleep to feel that he really would have got to the small park, to his assignation, if only he had stayed asleep just that bit longer, just until he got there, and she would have got there too, and at last this time... But he couldn't remember who it was in the dream. He had lost it, but the curves of the luscious blue and green fruit, the dark blue pears, carried the excitement from the island into the air above his coverlet, rich tapestried colours, the shapes of flowery Cockaigne. He woke and looked at the bed in the light of day coming through the window and they were pears most delicious hanging in the blue twisty trees; there were two pears in a window.

There were pale yellow pears on the kitchen window-sill on a square plate the bird and flower pattern of which was rubbed to a faded nothing against the cream ground. They had loved those plates with budgerigars and yellow and orange daisies on them, and this was the last old survivor from years ago. He put a cup of tea beside his wife, the coloured shapes on the coverlet now nestling with its weight round her sleeping form. He patted the thick down snugly round her lovely rump, liking the dry feel of the weave of the worn material, and in the kitchen took a pear with smooth pale skin mottled like a frog. It slithered when he tried to peel it, so he gulped it to catch the juice. It was cool and it was special to be eating the only ripe pear for breakfast. The juice ran down his chin, its fragrance on his tongue. He looked at the bend of the track as the train came travelling westwards along it into the station, filling the space above it with a snake of black. The steel of the track dazzled him and the edges of the black shape of the train pulsated with a great glow. Rocking and singing the train went on its usual journey into Town, and he with it.

He must get up soon but he didn't want to, though he wasn't comfortable. The tapestry coverlet gritted his skin when the back of his hand brushed against it. It was gloomily shabby. There was a greasy bald rim where all the people who had used it (and he as a child) had clutched the edge to accompany them into the land of dreams. They had both been pleased when his mother had given it them. If he'd had a dream last night he couldn't remember it, and if he'd had one it had not been a pleasing one. Perhaps a nice fresh cotton, a new duvet for Janet's birthday. Would she like that, though? Perhaps it was the closed room – stuffy and cold and maybe the onions that made him feel heavy. Up he got, brought Janet tea. There was a pear for his breakfast, especially for him from the last of what they'd stored. It didn't invite him. It was pale on a cracked cold plate. What a lot of effort they'd spent on their fruit trees. You could get better in the shops as cheap. As he peeled the pear it slid out of his fingers and fell with a dull splodge on to the floor. It was pappy – what was left of it by the time he'd washed it off. He cleared all traces away, not wanting his wife to know it hadn't been nice, leaving the table clean and uncrumby for her breakfast. The thought of her appreciating coming to a clean prepared breakfast-table usually gave him pleasure but it looked unappetising to him. As he got on the train the passengers slamming doors seemed particularly noisy today, his eyes smarted and the lurching carriage made him feel unwell.

Vice versa

They had had a book at home which was very clever. You looked at the pictures, through, one way up and they were all marvellously drawn heads, bushy eyebrows, wrinkled pates, creased chins, expressive eyes. Then if you turned it upside down you could start again and there they all were, the same pages, the same lines on the page, but this time they were not scowling unhappy faces. The domed foreheads had become pendulous chins, upper lips lower lips, whiskery beards sideburns, sunken faces turned into smiling ones.

The dream in the day

She had to get out of the hospital to ask advice. She dreamt she walked out with this intention and came to flooded streets so her way was halted. Her lover was there. It was sweet relief to see his tall thin figure. He was balding rapidly. Now there was no need for the impossible task of finding him. Now there was nothing to stop them from kissing. They had time to talk and they stepped inside the door of a hangar where there was quiet where they would be completely undisturbed. The preventing world had gone away, or they from it. In the corner just beside the door they kissed softly, his breath so sweet and his lips so soft. All was sureness now, it was peaceful there, they could leave the rest till later. Just this kiss now but everything ahead, nothing to stop them now. That was his unspoken assurance to her. His person there assured her. They were on their way, he would see to it.

Then they were in the light by a harbour side, she, she thought, going with him. Across the water, covering the hill on the other side of the semi-circular basin, were bright houses.

'There is my house and I'm going,' he said. She knew they would not meet again. Now they would never make love. She could ask quite boldly, because it was a dream, 'Why?' He started to answer: 'Because...' and she strained to catch the answer. To know the reason, to hear what he said was of the utmost importance. But the reason was drowned in the noise of the water, the water lying everywhere in the streets that she now noticed again for it was all around nosing into unused places where it had never been, trying this place and that like an uncertain dog. She found herself in other different parts of the town she had never been in, wading through fords which spilled and slapped and lapped further down the streets and up against walls. What worried her was that her best shoes were full of water. Because of this she made no progress. She was nowhere near where she had been trying to get.

She woke to the calm autumn day it was. Like the day it was some time before she quite came to. The dream wrapped her and she went into her day with it. They would not meet again or make love now.

On a sure slow-moving morning of autumn, a man with no urgency came out of his back door. He was not going to be rushed on such a day. He was going to savour the relaxation that surety gave. This still weather would last a long time. There was enough time. He took his time to look at a perfect web a little spider was building in the sparkling brambles. He saw that one or two of the filaments were not regular. There had been one or two little mends where the wind had swayed the pendulous fabric, heavy with wet, or a heavy insect had bumbled against it, breaking it.

Suddenly he wanted that the thread should be taken to its final point and knotted up. He urgently wanted the pattern to be complete, the circumference drawn so that the bull's eye could be centred and hit, love brought to its end. He couldn't bear for things to hang fire any longer, for the spider endlessly to continue at the same tempo, as when he, the man, had all the time in the world, as if there was that sort of time still. He had to dash in, put on his clothes and get to work. He could not unravel the threads to make them fit the pattern.

The web would get tatty and when the winds blew it would get pulled and stripped.

He left it. He and the fly were outside. They were in the sun.

Vice versa II

Some days it's clear at the top while the bottom is dark in mist, and someone travelling along the valley road to the town would not be aware that above that lid of thick air are sloped fields, sun on a yellow square, a brown one next to it, lightened clear patchwork with hedge lines running across the contours in a gentle swell; visible and actual to someone walking up there, a long light view through bare trees that ring the crest of the hill. So thick and close is the blanket of fog for those travelling along the valley, creeping through the murk, the horizon standing on the bonnet of the car, that there can be no idea of "up there" at all.

Another day you are stumbling down the wooded slopes, feeling your way by passing from one clung-to tree-trunk to another guessed at five feet away. You leave what you can see, or sense rather, for the surmised, as a non-swimmer might push off from the swimming pool steps to the helper standing within a torso's launch. Droplets of wet cling to your hair, dripping into your eyes, the wool of your scarf. Your breathing is painful in the clammy cold, eyes smart from the glare through which surges the illusion of a slight darkening, representing solid shapes, flashes but no sight. No sound gives direction. So dense and total the fog, it might be an ancient forest covering a quarter of England one is lost in, not a deciduous grove in winter on the side of a hill above a town. Any moment your foot will be over a cliff or quarry edge. Oh why did you leave the path thinking that straight down would get you to the bottom quickest? Night will come and you will still be here blundering about, hurt and frightened, cold and lost. Perhaps it is night now. It might as well be. With the next hesitant step you are as suddenly clear of it, for no reason, as you were suddenly engulfed. You are on level ground, can see your feet. You can see everything. You can see where you are. You can see.

The valley has been breathing blue air all this while in sunshine and the ice on the leaves and the puddles is melting.

Rose growing

Many times she had thought she ought to have that sucker up. It straggled and caught at her clothes whenever she wanted to work on the rose bed. It would bear no flowers. A good gardener would have not had to think before immediately extirpating it. It sapped the ground. No doubt it was preventing the rest from doing well. That it was still there, waving its shooting fronds over the path catching at her when she forgot to duck, was a mark of incompetence. The whole corner was a mess but each time she was about to have a go at it the fresh green leaves looked glossy, almost winked in their copper green lightness. The arc of stem was graceful on the breeze bobbing joyfully in its unkempt life. It was hard to destroy a healthy growth when there was not much else shooting up just then.

She had seen him in the Post Office about a year after she had known for good and all that he had left the town for good and all, and he had spoken as if he'd been away a week when she came up to him. 'I was coming round to see you. Will you be in tonight? I know I've still got some of your books. I'll bring them round at six if that suits you and we'll go and have a drink.' Same old gloss, same old sway in whatever breeze that was blowing, anything for the moment to catch the moment that passed. Same solitary night. Same silence at 6, 6.30, 7, 8, 9 until long after someone might be reasonably or unreasonably delayed. Same blank. Same lack of all prescience. And, whatever her knowledge told her, same occupation in her mind for weeks after; that corner of the chamber of the mind where possibilities are laid ready to hand like clean clothes, in case.

One day working with good effect on the garden, doing whatever came to hand towards the rose bed, in the normal course of jobs being done she rooted it up. It was next to her hand and up and out it came in her gloved hand. She raked all over and cleared to the bonfire pile and went in for some lunch. The whole Sunday morning and exhaustion and nothing else done, just to make a mess, she thought. When she came back she saw the bed was much improved and thus had an effect on the whole garden. A good morning's work. And the rose no loss, for its roots had been rotten and diseased. She should have pulled it up long ago.

She saw him and he didn't see her. He was going into the butcher's. The ill fit of his trousers on his short legs as he shambled, ordinary inhabitant stayed here in the town after all in a petty round, was what she noticed first. She was immensely relieved that she didn't need to do anything to avoid him; to avoid him not because she was overcome with feeling and she wished not to show it ridiculously in face of indifference, but avoid such blood-shot, dull-eyed lack-lustre, such heaviness. To have wished – longed for – such a drag...! Quick away. The air deadened in the street. She breathed with difficulty for a bit.

There were plenty of pretty things to go in that corner now that it was clear: stocks, dahlias; even a Chinese bush a friend had recommended that flowered in winter. Many alternatives now she had that space again. It would alter that part. There were more ways than one of having that corner.

Summer evenings sometimes took her walking to the bridge when the sun had left the sky but there was still light enough for outlines to be sharp and clear. They had met once by chance here, at the time when he had been enthusiastic, and they had walked up to the lock in the warm night air and swum and dried off on his shirt that smelt so nice and they had had a wonderful evening. Well, she was not denying anything. She could put herself in the way of circumstance if circumstance should present itself. You must use the summer while it's here. She came home through her night garden in the dusk almost intoxicated with the uninterrupted pleasure she'd had from her walk – all the sights and sounds by the river.

Even when the evenings drew in and there was not so much light between work and getting home she was often in the garden before turning in, to smell the night-scented flowers and to sense on the ground dusking at her feet especially the late white flowers growing there. Another good day stretched ahead tomorrow and she glad of it. It would have been nice, she agreed, to have had the velvety dark rose that had been suggested for that corner. It would have completed her idea of a garden and it would have been admired, but the other things did better there. It was her garden. It had to be as she could make and work it. She was obviously not a rose grower like Mrs Pettit. Well then, it was another sort of garden.

A couple for dinner

He knew he should try and get home at least promptly, with the wine bought. He could have done that in the lunch hour so that he could be clean and shaved, available in the hour before the couple who were coming to dinner arrived. She had been using every interval all week, buying a tin of cream where she could in case she couldn't get fresh on the day, up to the delicatessen where they ground the proper coffee she wanted so she wouldn't have to go up there in the crush on Friday, doing the washing and cooking after supper when he'd gone to bed, to release today for getting the house and meal ready. The more he thought of the evening the more his unwillingness for the endeavour made him incapable almost to the point of physical paralysis of doing anything about it. If he could have followed his instinct he would have disappeared for six to eight hours somewhere dim and solitary or anonymous like a station bar, as an animal burrows into the leaves under a hedge until a storm blows itself out.

His anxiety was partly on account of Cathy, his wife. 'There's no need to ask them to a meal,' he said. 'It was a children's party that Tony went to. You see – what's her name, the mother? Clarissa – when you pick him up from school. Just because Tone's been there you don't have to get out the family silver and have a dinner party to return hospitality. ('The family silver' was one of their family jokes. They hadn't any.) And their Bevis comes round here to play and have tea, doesn't he – nice little chap. We could take him with us next time we take Tone to the zoo.'

'I thought you liked them – you did enjoy it at their house when we went to pick Tony up, you know you did. I seem to remember we were the last to leave because you were ensconced so comfortably with Maurice although on the way you said we wouldn't stay so I hadn't changed. You didn't find him difficult to talk to did you?'

'Oh, they're a very attractive couple. I did like them. But it's a lot of work for you Cathy. I'm sure they don't expect – ' He couldn't say, 'We're just not in their class. We haven't got the resources. You'll make a fool of yourself,' far less admit, 'You'll show me up, reveal the shabbiness of my house and family, pushing our personal circumstances up the noses of people who needn't know them. You'll embarrass me. You can't go asking a couple like that to a place like this.'

'If I never make an effort we won't get to know anyone. After all, they were friendly enough to invite Tony. If Clarissa can do all that – wasn't it beautifully done with that basket of presents all wrapped up individually for the children to take home? And she told me they'd only just finished doing the bathroom the week before. They've done most of the work themselves in that house, you know. Maurice works long hours and she has no more time than I do. I think she does a part-time job as well as everything else. She goes up to Hornsey three times a week – either a course she's doing or hospital visiting or something. That's why she said Friday would be the best day for them. It was nice of them to say they'd like to come, I thought.'

A picture of Cathy in a dress that had been pretty ten years ago at the sort of gathering where everyone brought a tooth mug and a bottle of awful Spanish plonk, bringing in a brown casserole that was really old and cracked and not just of the newly-made, old-fashioned sort becoming available in Country Kitchen Supply Stores, Cathy making jokey apologies about the cutlery, made him stiff with embarrassment. Well, he'd have to get another sub. He couldn't get anything he wouldn't be ashamed to pour out in front of Maurice with even twice the money she'd given him to get the wine. He'd been given a glass of good Madeira at their house. At least Maurice should know that he knew what was what.

He'd got the sub at lunch time and of course bought Derek a drink for the favour, although he'd said he'd had enough and wanted to get back to work. Cathy just didn't understand the way you had to do things with these sort of people.

'Darling, can I leave the table to you? I've put everything in there – no don't open the fridge door, it's packed rather precariously. If you could see to the sitting room.' There was no shutting the door on the chaos of their narrow passage of a kitchen as their lavatory was in a cramped lobby beyond it. Oh, he was so slow when she could do with twice the number of hands and twice the time that was left. 'Your clean shirt's on the bed. I've ironed the blue one.' When he suggested a cup of tea and said that as they wouldn't be eating until after eight he'd better have a sandwich or something to keep him going, he hadn't had any lunch, she practically screamed.

'I'll just go and say goodnight to the children.' Cathy, bless her, was no good at ironing shirts. He'd nip up and do it properly.

She'd been getting on well until then. The children had been bathed early and helped her tidy away the more unwelcome traces of children's presences from the living room, hall, stairs and lavatory. The casserole was ready, the rice was on, the sprouts in salt water prepared, the soup more or less ready. Now that she could see her way clear again she was sorry she'd not been more sympathetic to Kenneth. She didn't want him feeling neglected because people were coming. 'Would you like some soup now if you're hungry, and you can tell me what it needs?' she shouted up the stairs. 'No I'll wait now.' As he came down she said encouragingly, 'That shirt does suit you.' She had spent more money than on the rest of Christmas on that shirt for him last year.

He had taken the table in and banked up the fire which was just getting going nicely. Catherine, praise be, had at last got a lampshade for their rickety standard lamp so they needn't have the centre light on. At least they had some decent glasses, a present Catherine's aunt had given her long ago. They'd need washing. 'Have you got a clean tea-towel?'

Quarter to eight. With any luck they wouldn't be here jump on eight. Fifteen minutes to change. 'Darling, could you see if my black shoes are in the back room? Behind the door?'

By five past eight she'd brushed her hair, put on some lipstick, stowed away dirty towels from kitchen and bathroom, dusted the hall table leaving just a few books and a plant. The next ten minutes gave her time to put the plates in the oven, get clean towels and apron, make a space in the cupboard to hang coats up, find a clothes brush and get the cat litter out of the kitchen. Kenneth rubbed up her shoes. She even dawdled a little tidying up their bedroom after the frantic disarray of finding clothes, put on some eye-shadow she came across and a brooch she'd wanted to wear. She put some cream on her stinging rough hands and feeling more comfortable felt more presentable.

At half past eight there was the worry as to whether they should ring the couple – perhaps Clarissa even now, let down by a baby-sitter, was searching for their telephone number. On no account would Kenneth allow it. It would be highly embarrassing. Was Cathy sure she'd asked them for this Friday? Was Cathy sure they'd said they'd come? He could imagine her saying, trying to be casual, 'Do drop in if you're doing nothing on Friday, and have a bite to eat – nothing formal.' Diffident, inelegant Cathy giving them a let-out, which obviously they'd taken. The rice was congealing, the kitchen steamed up. Cathy really had had no lunch or even ten minutes sit-down with a cup of tea. The tiredness kept back by the stimulation of necessity now swept over her. What a waste, what a failure. What a fool she'd made of herself. She'd turned the whole week and more than a fortnight's money round this dinner party. A very dreary evening stretched ahead. If they came now she'd be too tired to make conversation or even know what she was doing. If they didn't Kenneth would go to bed early and she'd spend the night putting everything back.

'Come and sit down and have a drink, Cathy. You might as well. If we're all relaxed and started they won't feel awkward at being a bit late.' 'Just a sip then,' she was still anxious there should be enough wine to be lavish to guests. She noticed a plant that needed water and a floorcloth by the fire place. 'Madam, your health,' Kenneth said as she came back. He was quite a good mimic when loosened a little with drink. 'You should dress up a bit more often. That eye-shadow suits you.' 'Mm, this is nice wine. I needed that.' The room was warm and welcoming, the lamp-shade she'd got that morning from a charity shop looked good away from the other junk, the table almost sparkling. They hadn't done badly. A pity the people they'd done it for wouldn't see it. Kenneth's eyes were beginning to close from the wine and the warmth.

'Well, let's eat,' she said suddenly. 'I'm starving.' They had every special thing. Cathy had even put mustard in the blue glass container in the silver filigree stand and found a mustard spoon from somewhere. She didn't put away the expensive decorated napkins or save for another festive occasion any other of the delicacies not normally for family consumption. As well as the wine after the trifle which she covered with glacé cherries and cream that she would normally have been delighted to be able to salvage and store, they finished up what remained in the bottle of liqueur Cathy's father had given them last Christmas.

They went more than a little tipsily up to bed. 'We must have people to dinner more often,' he said. 'That was a lovely meal.' 'It's a rather expensive way of getting the place clean. Will I have to ask people in every time I want help in the house?' 'No, it would do if we just thought they were coming. I'm going to pretend I've just met you at a wonderful dinner party and charmed you into bed with me.' He took her wedding ring off her finger and hid it behind the clock. 'And I'll act as if I would,' she said, ready for banter and talk and love after the success of the evening, but as she spoke she realised that he was already asleep.

The assignation

The girl was restless in the fine spring evening. She would have liked an assignation or even an errand. She'd seen to everything her grandmother needed. The evening lay all open.

She was just back for a fortnight's holiday this time, she told the welcoming people who'd known her as a child. She was doing agency nursing now, she said. Yes, it did give her more freedom. It had been a hard winter, Mr Maine at the Post Office told her, and spring was a tricky time for the old. He was glad to think Mrs Kemp would have someone to look after her for a bit. 'It's more likely to be her looking after me,' Sarah said. 'You know what she's like.' 'Yes, but what a wonderful woman.' No, thank you for enquiring, but he was sorry to say Mrs Maine wasn't too hearty at the moment. She hadn't really been over her bronchitis when that foreign flu came along. 'Still, we keep going. Got to, haven't we? I don't suppose they'll keep the Post Office open once we've gone.'

She went into the garden – plenty to do there – and heard the bells. Of course, it was Friday, bell-ringing practice. She hadn't kept up with the church group apart from going with her friend Betty to the carol services those Christmases she wasn't away on duty at the hospital. If her grandmother in her early days had attended any place of worship she had anyway been a Baptist. But the church was activity. If only there had been someone to say as she went lively and friendly on her errands here and there during the day, 'Walk up here in the evening and I'll meet you after bell-ringing practice,' and they could have gone through the church-yard to the stile at the bottom, the cluster of friends and fellow bell-ringers dispersing home to supper. She could suggest the high path through the woods. They could see if there were primroses, show him the quarry, the haunts and shelters she played in as a child and later mooned in on solitary walks dreaming of ardent companions. Of course when she did meet young men who were keen to get their arms round her it was in a borrowed car parked in some suburb cul-de-sac or round the back of a derelict ware-house that they went. The feverish associations readily available at the hospital with rushed housemen high on coffee, alcohol, lack of sleep and cigarettes, snatching at sensation to keep them going instead of proper food and sleep, had no place in them for Sunday outings and rambles.

Earlier she hadn't been able to get out of the chemist's, where she'd gone to fetch Gran's tablets, quickly enough when a new pharmacist helping in the dispensary while Mr Thurgood was recovering from an operation had asked how long she was here for, told her how much her grandmother had been looking for-ward to her visit and said how interesting it was for him to meet other people in the 'caring' professions and how lucky he felt he was to have the opportunity of getting to know such a beautiful part of the country. He'd come from Birmingham. He said, 'See you again,' rather loudly through the dispensary hatch as she went. Poor boring anxious man practising 'patient communication rela-tionships' from the latest training package, she'd thought, but now as if with a purpose, she walked up that way. One chemist in the area stayed open till after the doctor's evening surgery finished. Being a conscientious newcomer with no family to go home to perhaps he had lingered. But the chemist's was shut as was everything except the newsagent's where the owners of the three huge motorbikes parked outside were buying cigarettes and cans of fizzy drinks.

As she stopped to look at the astounding machines, padded, shiny, powerful, blocking people's way along the pavement, their owners came out. The one whose machine she was standing near was extremely attractive, a neat lean straight body and light eyes in a smooth olive face. If she praised his bike perhaps that taut curve of a well-shaped mouth which she couldn't take her eyes off would smile, he would have to look at her. And she would answer with as blatant a look. Perhaps if he'd been on his own he'd have talked to her, wanted to give her a ride on his motor-bike. No drag, she, to the lads. She'd show she was on their side against the old fuddy-duddies. Although cased in leather and barricaded by visored helmets they dressed and walked to convey the strength of their long thighs, the rippling of tight firm skin across their rib cages and shoulder blades. He bent to the bike to ease it off the kerb. At the same time as she opened her mouth – to say something, anything to make him acknowledge her presence (but what came out was a rather sharp 'A blind person might have quite an accident bumping into that') – he took off his helmet to settle it more comfortably and she realised how young he was, a schoolboy. He blushed up to his hairline and pursed his mouth. He glared at her from those extraordinary eyes and roared off after his friends.

There were three people as well as the vicar in the church porch chatting and smoking. The vicar smiled welcomingly at her as she came through the gate. Had she come to join their little band? New, especially young, members were most welcome, most needed now the older ones weren't getting any younger, but he was afraid they were just packing up for this evening. No, she said, she was just walking. But she loved hearing the bells and she did hope they'd keep it up. Perhaps they could look forward to seeing her in church on Sunday? The vicar had a sweet smile and obviously put himself at the service of his flock but his flock was small and dull and his personality diffident. He stooped sideways, being tall and thin and tried to keep in place with a frequently smoothing hand straggly thin hair. He was trying to remember whether he ought to recognise her. Was she that niece his churchwarden's wife was so proud of, come to look for her uncle? A lovely girl, anyway, very nice-mannered and interested. What a pity there weren't more like her around. With some jokes to the group about trying bell-ringing one day she went off through the churchyard over the stile and down towards the woods.

The track she took went in a great horseshoe above what was a stream now and a steep-sided ditch in summer. It emerged into the road only a few yards further on to where she'd left it. There were primroses. There was the nutty smell of beech mast stirred by her feet, there were scutterings, perpetual business in undergrowth, on the ground, in the trees, in the air. Birds were flitting along her route as if to lead her, but a route high above her head from tree to tree. There were ripples and movements in the banks overhung with fallen branches. There was so much to look at more closely, there was so much ahead she wanted to explore. There was also the cottage at the bend. When she saw the olive green sports car, and the car-port where the hen-run had been, and a new fence, she realised that she'd come this way with the thought of seeing old George. Old already he had seemed to her when, about nine, she had come and played in his wood when she was staying with her Gran during school holidays. He had first given her biscuits and something he called cherryade when she'd banged her knee one day falling from a rotting dead tree that had fallen across the stream and was slippery with moss. He'd taken her into his kitchen to wash the cut and comfort her. Now even his cottage and wood pile and ancient truck had gone.

Either way back would be quite far enough now. She'd like to be getting home. She went into the pub at the cross-roads, not to seek company but because she was tired and thirsty and no longer restless. She struck up a conversation with the landlord about the tree-cutting and fencing going on up the hill which she wanted to know about. When he asked her to have another, this time on him, she didn't want to linger, though another time, she said, she'd certainly like to. And when he said, 'Go on, a small one won't hurt, what's the hurry?' she felt a certain urgency, not so much to get home and be opening the front door and calling 'Gran' – her Gran wouldn't be worried – as to be on her way, with the hoard of her evening to savour, as when you want to get a new purchase home to unwrap it. She went that little bit brisker for there were assignations ahead these spring days, off exploring and noticing and stopping and thinking and taking in the evening. Tomorrow a friend of Gran's was coming, but her next free evening…

Roundabout

They would not diminish their own or each other's lives by pretending each was the other's answer, only answer, but neither could they leave; hoping the other would somehow become so, each wanting so much to have found an answer.

One night he was going to see her and he got deterred in by-roads. It was foggy and he lost all sense of direction along the unfamiliar route, where there were road-ups and diversions which confused him. Twice he emerged from a road that led by the side of a fir plantation – a dark vague bulk in the woolly dark – on to a major junction, or he thought it was the same place but it might have been a similar lie of the land further along. When for the third time he came back to a small mounded roundabout which she had described as the landmark to look out for, with a drooping utterly still birch tree on it only just discernible vaguely in the middle, he drove straight down the road he had come up, home. He took the phone off the hook and wrote her a note explaining how he'd tried several times to find the way but that when he saw the damned tree for the third time that decided him and he expected she'd realised about the fog and had probably given him up anyway by then and gone to bed.

Time maybe

'It is like when you're holding your breath so as not to mist the glass,' you said, 'and you are waiting for the moment you can release it.'

'What is?' I asked and you said, 'What is what?'

'You said "It's like". What's "it"?'

And I can see now your changed look, how you pulled your gaze back from the bit of the table you were looking at, in to the circle of our heads and hands where we sat talking over breakfast. You seemed halted, confined, and your face dimmed as when a shaft of light is prevented by a block from reaching its full extent. Then you picked up again. 'The dawn coming, or just before – that bit sleepy slug-a-beds like you never see,' and laughed and kissed.

But that wasn't what you meant and later when we came back alone into the house from a walk, for the others had left, you said 'No, I meant not just the dawn. Later in the day too. The presence of the day perhaps. It's probably something quite simple like the effect of light on certain spaces but I suppose that's what I think ghosts might be, a feeling of something there, something happening almost. Don't you ever get that feeling for a second when you come into a room and it's empty, that there's something waiting – not anything ominous, the opposite of frightening? Something you've disturbed. Time, maybe.'

In those days there was always family, friends, colleagues, the public. An empty house to me was a cold house, a bleak place, comfort withdrawn; absence of someone like you to light it up, to welcome me; no one to expect me.

In these changed circumstances now, unpacking long ignored boxes of old possessions, all that remained to me, I came across a worn green book, its spine so rubbed I had to open it to read what it was. It was your Emerson which you must have lent me, perhaps hoping to provide me with the necessity to visit you again, or you the excuse to ask for it back, your *Selected Verse and Prose of Emerson* which I had neither bothered to read nor returned. In contrition for my neglect, soft with self-pity, I started to look at it. I read:

> Daughters of Time the hypocritic Days,
> Muffled and dumb like barefoot dervishes,
> And marching single in an endless file
> Bring diadems and faggots in their hands.
> To each they offer gifts after his will,
> Bread, kingdom, stars and sky that holds them all.
> I, in my pleached garden, watched the pomp,
> Forgot my morning wishes, hastily
> Took a few herbs and apples, and the Day
> Turned and departed silent. I, too late,
> Under the solemn fillet saw the scorn.

There was a piece of paper marking the page on which was written in faded pencil:

'The days are ever divine...they come and go like muffled and veiled figures sent from a distant friendly party; but they say nothing, and if we do not use the gifts they bring, they carry them as silently away.' Works and Days. Emerson.

Could I, even this late, in this new abode that seems so cheerless, so empty, so bare of memories or possibilities, could I learn to recognise its ghosts, its presences – perhaps by noticing a simple thing like the effect of light on certain spaces?

Valley filled with rain

He had been ill and disappointed for a long time. He had gradually withdrawn from the groups and activities in his parish that he had tried to be part of when his family began to focus their lives elsewhere. He had not got another dog when Flora was run over. He began to think of himself as only really comfortable in his own house.

One winter afternoon of a day that was passing from the dark of a wet morning into another night without much breath or light to open the intervening hours, he found himself walking down the unmade road that led on to a patch of open ground on the side of the estate not yet built on. It petered out at a mesh wire fence where there'd once been a footpath round the side of the hill. He wasn't sure what had got him out there, interrupting his programme of domestic Sunday afternoon comforts. The valley he gazed at as he pressed against the wire was filled with rain. The cloud was clinging halfway down the hill and visibility was very low on this dark wet afternoon, but the air within it was rather refreshing. It was a long time since he'd walked in the rain, a long time since he'd just walked with no errand. Through the misty air he could make out roads criss-crossing the slope opposite. One or two tail lights of cars went busily up to a high flat area where they converged. He imagined them pausing, almost saluting, and then passing other cars making their way back across to this side as if they were part of some dance. It was a nexus, a crossing-point, a gathering, a congruence.

What a busy world it was over there just beyond the edge of visibility where the lights suddenly blinked out, hidden by the brow they were going over and on down the hill to emerge again further along the ridge. The fog-filled trench of the valley lay between. There was all that plain with farms, houses, lights to explore. Such concourse bringing people together elsewhere. For a time the invisible life seemed enticing, as when one hears band music several streets away on a hot stale August night in a town. But the path petered out. He had enjoyed his walk, the quiet refreshment and the dimness and the peace and he would go back home now and put the kettle on and read the paper. Perhaps he would get a dog in the spring – but not yet. It was getting bleak and would soon be quite wet and cold out here. By the time he reached home it was properly dark, and he glad not to be out in it any longer. With gratitude and pleasure he opened the door. The house too was a nexus, of the tracks through the days and the years people had made by living in it. It was warm and quiet. It sheltered him as the valley filled with rain.

Time waiting

As when a dog or child dashes beyond the ball it is after and finds itself briefly bewildered on a patch of empty grass, so expectation sometimes runs ahead of its object.

She came back into the house in the afternoon. It had been a proper Saturday full of bustle and then out into the town, here and there, part of the throng, all her clearing, cleaning, preparation, shopping, errands, moving towards that point when she would stow her bags on the corner bench inside the open door of the pub and be greeted by her friends. Morning having been achieved, the afternoon and evening it was opening out to invited. What she liked but it happened rarely was for the others to have only just got there, or to come in looking out for her, for them not to be going almost as soon as she'd at last sat down to stay a while; to be looked for.

As she went to her own door under a verandah at the side of the rambling house her anticipations quickened. Now for the – but what? Treat? From the camaraderie at the pub they had all gone – to the match, or home to families where dinner was ready, on outings, on assignations, expected, waited for, by other people. No one was going to call round. She had not arranged anything for the evening. She had wanted to keep her free day clear. For what, now tired, she could not think. She quickened at the thought of tea, but that was not what she'd come home so eagerly for. Should she ring Culver? She could write to Bea. She could alter her dress, that would fill in the time usefully, or she could take the curtains to the cleaners after tea. They were still open till six and it would save time on Monday. But that was ridiculous. She'd been doing things to save time at the weekend all week. That was not what she'd looked forward to getting home for.

She took her tea to the top room which Jo occupied when he used to come and stay. It looked over the side of the house, under the gable away from the road. She watched a child manoeuvring a tricycle over planks and stones in the back garden. There was of course not a message like she'd sometimes find – and which something in her could not quite get used to not hoping for – telling her what he was doing and when she could expect him or where to meet him; nor the signs that act as messages to people who share a life – which clothes they've discarded, what equipment picked up.

So it was the activity around her in the town and the stimulation of friends' company that had given her day its zest, suggesting promise of more of the same; and that had happened. It was not ahead. And the relish with which she came into the house for the best bit of the day, leaving the merry-go-round getting fainter behind her, was then just a habit, a survival of a trace that habit had laid in her nerves as irrelevant to present Saturdays as an appendix. She looked ahead not at a lake shimmering with unexplored islands but an uninterrupted desert of afternoon evening night morning afternoon evening to be got across till work again on Monday. Well, it was still pleasant in the house. She would get things done. She would write to Bea.

She didn't start her letter or read the paper she'd brought in and as she drank tea and rested and the outside world ebbed she started to listen to the house. She realised the place was not empty. The light shifted in the room, the day moved gradually over the walls and ceiling and had been doing so since early morning, and all week, and all the time since she'd been up here. The house made no claim until she was free to perceive it but it was there. And the life in it, all that had gone on in it, – that the house was keeping for her for when she should come. It was waiting, as expectant, she felt, as she was. Though nothing happened, no message, no one called, it was as if the people who'd been there, the things they'd done, the times they'd been together, filled the room;

as if someone was waiting for you, the emptiness, the absence

as if someone had been there, leaving the trace of their company, their welcome, a smile to mirror hers, leaving something to mark their place like a slip of paper in a book. That was what she'd hastened in to get, that was the visitor she didn't want to miss: the life in the house before the day took it once more untasted.

As a book holds the life that went into it long ago, which, seeming to pass, is left in store for when someone shall come and open it and release it and make a channel for it again, so what the house had stored it held for her. She would not even turn the light on as it grew dusk lest she disturb the assignation she had kept. The place was full after all. She had come to a meeting and by no means had come in to nothing. It was full of time.

Widower

He had expected to go first. It had been his health not hers that had caused concern; it was a new life for him, after his heart attack, after he'd lost his job, that they had worked for.

When he went into the town after that he was reduced to being a tripper drifting around looking for ways to use up the weekday hours, just a shopper struggling back on the bus in the afternoon with the schoolchildren and the OAPs, before the workforce flowed down the arteries of the place for that humming time of vigour and expectation concentrated between leaving work and getting home.

As if his back bone had been taken out, the network his existence at the printing works provided had disappeared. Rather, he felt that he had disappeared. The solider part of his life, the job, had remained, but he was exiled from it.

At first he'd looked into the Works on days he went into the town, but he depended on Bertha to drop him there. Then, in the months before they shut down completely, the few who still worked there became preoccupied and worried and hurried and not much interested in being sociable over a beer and a sandwich with someone sunk into the position they dreaded for themselves, one of the down and going, not the up and coming that their instincts impelled them towards.

So this is old age and illness, this is being at the end of the line, this is it, he had realised.

That had been five years ago and, until Bertha died, to recall the emptiness, the disappointment, the disagreeableness, the sourness he had felt, he had to make an effort, so different had his life become. It was like trying to feel the paralysis of cold when one is luxuriating in balmy summer nights. He'd done pretty well to create a new life for himself after he'd had to retire.

Yes, he'd done a pretty good job. He'd found out how to turn ploys to seem busy into real activities he came to enjoy. They formed a basis for an occupied life in the way a wire mesh will hold concrete. He had constructed it, piece by piece as when you begin to set a course of bricks, bringing a few at a time from a rubbish dump, or like Bertha's knitting, stitch by stitch, then back again at the same speed, fiddling until there was enough fabric to shape a form. At the time of Bertha's death he was so occupied – they had plans for eighteen months ahead – their son in Australia had at last persuaded them to accept the present of the air-fare out there to visit him. He wouldn't have had time to do a job now, he used to say, wouldn't want his old job back even had it been on offer, not even the position he should have had in the firm that had swallowed up Dick and Olafson.

He had built up a life again from blank, from near death once (his heart attack) twice (what he'd thought of as a sort of death at the time of his redundancy). He'd thought so, till now. He could not do it yet again with Bertha gone. 'Gone,' he said but it remained a mournful word. Even after two and a half months something in his body couldn't realise that he would never again see her, hear her, smell her, touch her – no, those were surface things – feel her to be there. She wouldn't ever be there again. He supposed, as neighbours had said, that her dying suddenly meant it took longer for it to sink in. Tears of weakness and self-pity overcame him as her name came into his thought. He was standing in the kitchen looking at the shelf with tins of different teas in, about to make a pot of tea, which he would probably leave unpoured until in an hour or so he emptied it out to make a fresh pot, or if poured, leave standing in the cup till cold and scummy. The joke that used to amuse him about Colman's making their fortune out of the mustard people left on the side of their plates drifted across his brain but merely depressed him.

All his actions, such words as he spoke and those of others he heard, he felt were a foot or two outside his body, as if he were encased in a diver's helmet and nothing could get through directly to his brain, his heart, his guts, his blood flow. When he did register seeing things again they were without colour, distant and yet oppressive, as if you were to walk out and there was no weather in the streets. Although he wept at the sound of her name whether he or anyone else produced it he wasn't thinking about her. He could recall nothing about her. Impressions and images of her were unattainable, even further than the foot or two outside his skin where the world went on.

He pushed the chair out from under the table with his foot, sullenly and more clumsily than necessary, and sat on it to give in to his shaking sobs. He could not be expected to do it again. There was no reason for trying. What was there to try for? What was it he was meant to want to do?

For some time after the boy had gone back to Australia, after the funeral, he had accepted invitations from the kind and efficient people of Bertha's acquaintance. He felt like a child who couldn't bear to be left on his own in a strange place, yet all the time he sat in busy kitchens, sat on after the meal they had given him, watched television with them, played snap with their children, he felt he should be going, that there must be things he should be doing. He couldn't get used to having nothing to leave for nor think that it wasn't intolerable for people to have him hanging around with his grief and confusion, burdening the atmosphere, for it was intolerable to himself.

Then he felt he was boring them, not so much in wanting to go on about Bertha whatever pretext he had visited on, but in not continuing to talk about the things they were ready to listen to, had got ready to offer comfort on. Instead he had latterly insisted on dragging up all that about his heart attack. 'Now you don't want to dwell on all that old stuff. You were never ungrateful to Bertha. You always acknowledged how much she did. You don't want to start feeling guilty about things Bertha would never have thought of. I can tell you for a fact that she was glad when you started to rely on her. You'd always seen to everything. She had a lot of hidden talents your wife. She really came into her own those last years. What she most wanted was to be of help. And you know you weren't always an easy man to help, George.' 'Oaf,' he thought. He glared and muttered to himself through clenched teeth, 'They were not hidden,' at the same time knowing the speaker was only trying to be 'of help'.

Why would people not believe him, not listen to what he was saying? He wasn't trying to say he hadn't realised Bertha's worth, that he'd not appreciated her until she wasn't there. He didn't feel guilty. They had urged him to talk about his feelings, his state; had persuaded him, against the habit of his temperament, that it was good to talk it out; not to be so controlled or think he was troubling people with his trouble. Now that there was something he was eager to unburden himself of they wouldn't listen. They chewed over the same comments: that because she'd gone so suddenly it was more of a shock, that of course it was more difficult for it to sink in when a death was sudden but how much better what a mercy that, if it was to be, it was sudden with no suffering; that she wouldn't have wanted him to neglect himself, would have wanted him to go on with his life as fully as possible as she'd encouraged him to do after his heart attack. And there was no doubt that he had said all these things too, called round on friends, stayed late into the evening with people he'd called on just to give them something from the garden, or some memento of Bertha more of use to them than to him, and really wouldn't come in this time, or only for ten minutes then. Whatever he'd set out to do he found himself doing anything than go home to an empty house, or rather, to one full of furniture and stuff and absence. He couldn't blame them for missing the point when he had – all these years.

It came as a shock and was the first thing for months he'd found interesting. It was an important and interesting discovery that made things clear, even if he couldn't make it clear to others, as a torch, flashed on a dark road, shows up an outline which you then take account of even after the instant of clarity is swallowed by obscurity again. It was this: he had got the past wrong.

It wasn't just that, as Bertha wasn't there, there was nothing to get over his misery at her death for, in the way that he'd had to make efforts to minimise his depression when he was ill so as not to add to her burden of worry. Couldn't they see? How could he get over her death since what her death meant was she wasn't there to help him get over her death?

It was all very well for neighbours to say – but it was his effort they were talking about. They weren't going to do it. He'd got to. So if it was only for him to do or not do, he hadn't got to. After his heart attack and redundancy it had been Bertha's effort. She didn't give advice. She didn't encourage people to do this or that. In fact she discussed very little. She'd gone about getting him involved in things, arranged needs, made demands on him, she who had taken care not to do that for herself. She invited, got him invited, asked favours of him for her friends and the club, arranged possibilities.

The sleights and ploys whereby Bertha had helped him to create a new life for himself when the old one dropped away were of not the slightest use now. The main thing being that she wasn't there to effect it. The main thing, in fact, not being. Any idea of recovery was hopeless, and to struggle for it in the way they were beginning to suggest he should was a useless thing to try to do. Bertha had gone and she wouldn't ever be there again. He was alone. She didn't exist anywhere. He saw it now. It had been her not him who'd put him back into the world of necesssities and responsibility, wound him with threads as light and functional as spider silk. She had attached him to the life of the place and given him a position in it.

Well, but his connection with the design department at the technical college, their neighbour Jessie's need for help with her garden, being treasurer of his local's Christmas club, the outings that the Gorleston Men's Sports and Social Club organised for the children's home every summer, even the talks he'd given (and been paid for) on how to prepare for approaching retirement at a 'weekend workshop' funded by the firms who were wanting to shed employees, need not stop. These were things he did quite separately from Bertha. Although of course they did much more together now than when he was working, the habits of thirty years had not altogether changed. They were not the sort of couple who did everything in tandem.

This was going through his mind one night when he was locking up, putting their two cups ready for the tea he, from a lifetime of early rising, would take up in the morning. 'You've got to face reality,' the words of the doctor who'd advised him to accept redundancy came into his head, in his own voice. He must stop his body, which could not supply him with any active memory of Bertha, behaving as if she were still there and would effect the cure. They were right. He must pull himself together and live in the present with real people.

He put the cups away carefully, then violently kicked over the rubbish bin, threw what was on the table into the sink so that the crockery broke, and went to bed.

He stopped doing all the jobs he'd busied himself with, even those he'd always done in the house. He'd been a tidy man. His apprenticeship as a printer had taught him that, and his father. He'd been in the Merchant Navy and took him camping one glorious summer and showed him how to get the most out of a bucket of water. It was strange, now that he was in his mother's predicament of being widowed, his parents, whom he had not really thought of for years, began to come into his mind more.

Now he did nothing – left food going bad in the fridge and cupboards, did nothing about the increasing signs of mice, didn't light a fire when he was cold or heat the water but just went to bed, lying on top in his clothes with a car blanket and an eiderdown wrapped round him.

One day he had to go to the bank and the solicitor. He cleaned himself up a bit for this. Having no clean shirt he got out a new one from the cupboard with the reserve tea towels and other things Bertha stocked up with at the January sales. When he put the water heater on for a bath something of their old domestic habits together flickered for an instant, for they used to do everything that needed hot water either first thing in the morning or last thing at night (when Bertha had her bath). She thought they saved electricity that way. So there came into his mind an image of him reaching for the washing-up liquid over a sink filling with hot water, ringing out cloths, swabbing down, while his bath ran, and he would have liked to have started on a thorough clear-up now instead of going into the town, so that the house would be 'nice to come into' when he got back. For a second he saw the house in its mess as someone coming in from outside might have done and a little shame, and sorrow for the house, woke in him, but he took a long time over his ablutions, having to look for nail scissors, shampoo and clothes and shoe polish and in the end, exhausted, had to rush if he was to catch a bus in time to keep his appointment.

Coming out of the bank he bumped into his friend Thompson. They had been old drinking mates and gone to football matches together long ago. Thompson had been father of the Chapel when he was secretary in the days when the Works and the Union were busy and vigorous when they lifted the quota rationing. Of course there had been jokes about him being a 'father' as, even in his thirties, he'd looked a slim lad not long out of school. He had left the trade long before George, travelled round a bit, made a lot of money working for an engineering firm out in the desert and on his return bought himself into the pub trade.

A lecherous, kind and responsible Scot who never let his bouts of heavy drinking interfere with his business, he had not seen George since the funeral, for family life and family friends take over at times of family bereavement. George and Thompson could and did discuss with ease matters of sex and women, moral and personal situations, that they would not have where the relation-ship was more closely dependent and where frankness about their feelings would have likely brought misapprehension.

Thompson would and did understand what George had to say about his growing desperation that he felt nothing about Bertha. He took him to have lunch across the road from the bank, not in his own pub, listened to him and made sure he had something to eat with his beer.

It wasn't his devotion to Bertha's memory that kept him reclu-sive in the house, George explained, and it was no good suggest-ing he should start to get back into life, because he hadn't the spunk, he had never had the spunk to get up after a fall. It had been Bertha not him all those years that had effected that. Even that part of him – those longings, attractions, leanings towards what would have hurt Bertha, his involvment in things utterly contrary to their way of life – his gambling, his unreliability when

136

his son had gone to Australia when she needed him most, his desire to be unfaithful, his wistful envy of people – him, Thompson, for instance – who were free to let cock follow where cunt beckoned – yes, he groaned, there had been times when he'd wanted rid of Bertha's understanding love, oh not for any harm to come to her, but to be free, not to be beholden, perhaps for her to be indifferent and neglectful or difficult so he could slip into looser ways with no burden on his conscience. Thompson understood that you could love someone and have a happy marriage and also feel these things; but now that he was free there was nothing he wanted to do. It was literally that he had no spunk. He couldn't remember what it was like to feel the least sexual stirring. He had no hunger but was all the time empty and he was aware of the emptiness with a numbness that caused him as much distress as pain. Drinking made him feel sick and then go to sleep, tired but no rest. He'd swing to extremes, he said, had grandiose plans which would solve his life, throwing off in one go the problems of what to do with their house, their things, the days, the years, himself, and within minutes sink into a state where the thought, even, of lifting a spoon to his mouth was too much and he would put it down in the bowl of congealing food and just sit until he could heave himself up to bed.

Thompson asked him to come and give him a hand the following evening. He had a wedding party to look after in the club room. He had reliable staff but it would help to have a friend around downstairs.

'Luckily I've got Margaret back. Lucky for me, that is. Not so much for her. Going back to that horrible husband of hers didn't work I'm afraid. I could have told her, but she wanted to go. Poor girl, if ever a woman deserved better that one does. You two always had a good time together. You could help each other now. She's longing to have someone decent to look after.' 'I'm not decent,' George said. 'No, but you're more decent than her old man. She asked after you – would have sent her condolences or called round. She's perking up a bit now, now she's where she's appreciated. Goodness, you should have seen the state she was in when she first turned up again, jumping and dithery whenever a door banged. Talk about nerves! She's a good lass, and fond of you. Give it a try. If you come about seven that'll be early enough. I'll get the shelves all bottled up. You won't have to lift anything, just have a good time and be there if the staff need you.'

He went with Margaret once or twice partly because he felt it benefited him to get back to a normal physical life and because he didn't want to give a direct slap in the face to a young woman full of loving feelings.

She was longing to look after him, to supply his lacks, his loss and in letting her, wanting her to, he would supply hers. In the old days they had had an understanding that they would both like to get to bed together if ever the circumstances allowed.

He made excuses about not asking her to the house, not letting her look after him there: (he wanted to give her a night out not more work, the house was in no fit state to be visited, he could do with getting out of the house himself) and then, too kind and too cowardly to tell her the truth – that it bored him, that her gasps and her rubbings and her reachings for him and her praise and admiration and encouragement for his prowess as a lover turned him off rather than on, he hinted that it wasn't fair on her, that what she needed was a younger man. (Whereas he knew that what she wanted was him and it was him that needed an older woman. How perverse I am, he thought. Most men my age in my situation wouldn't believe their luck.) So he told Margaret what he knew was a hurtful lie. 'I still don't feel like anyone, you know, disturbing Bertha's things.' He was playing on her tact. 'I didn't know you believed in ghosts,' she said, sharpened by the rebuff. 'No I didn't think I did either. It isn't quite that.' 'You were prepared to be unfaithful to her when she was alive, and left me to look after your conscience for you by saying no. Now, when she can't benefit from your consideration, now you're prepared to be scrupulous.' 'I'm sorry, Margaret. You're right of course. It's just selfishness. Men are.'

He didn't believe in ghosts and he didn't care about the house. Bertha was not on his mind. He felt mean about Margaret but mostly relief that she was not there with him in his squalid kitchen and dirty bed.

Nor, when it came to it, did he want to move in with Jessie. There had been times, when he was swinging to and fro like an unsecured boom in a wind, that he felt he would do almost anything not to be alone, not to have to decide about his life. After his son John had left, having failed to persuade him to go back with him to Australia, he had had attacks of great regret that he had said no. One very grim evening he was on the way to the phone. John had begged him not to feel he couldn't change his mind, he only had to ring. He was a good boy. He'd been very close to his mother. As he lifted the receiver to dial he was overcome with the paralysis of dread. He put it down quickly before he had to speak and left it off the hook purring and clicking all night. The flicker of energy that had made him grasp at action seemed to have been used up in thinking of phoning. The next time the ache to be rid of his situation became acute he told himself that he could still write to the boy and suggest a visit. When he envisaged the reality, the thought of having to talk to strangers on the journey, let alone be stuck perpetually day after day every minute of his life in a life that wasn't his, overcame him with lassitude.

With the effort of a schoolboy he was keeping up Bertha's habit of a weekly letter because he knew John and Alice would worry about him if they didn't hear and perhaps start ringing up or keeping in touch through Jessie. He wrote saying he was gradually getting through the business of sorting out Mother's things. In fact he was doing less and less even to keep the house inhabitable.

He went on working in Jessie's garden, though. She thought she was providing him with an anchor, an easy way of seeing her. He was grateful but by now he kept it up for Jessie's and Bertha's sake. At first he'd thought he'd got comfort from being in a place Bertha had known so well, from seeing some of the things she'd given Jessie, and the photograph, on the mantelpiece together with those of Jessie's long dead husband and her daughter and grandchildren in Germany, of Jessie and Bertha together, as they often had been. They'd had it taken on a trip to the seaside, not this seaside on the east coast where, separately, they'd come to live later, but a holiday seaside in the West Country. Jessie had offered it to him but though it was charming – two giggling girls enjoying themselves – he'd said, no, you keep it. He didn't want photographs of her, her soft round face and vitality so uncannily looking at him and so unreachably far, so painfully absent never to be regained, and, how much sharper the pang for this lost world of Bertha's youth which he had never known.

He had thought he would get Jessie to talk about Bertha, which she was only too ready to do, at the time when he could not remember much and could not think about her. Perhaps Jessie knew some of the things Bertha had kept from him. But they were only ordinary things he could have guessed for himself and he learnt more about Jess than Bertha. Apart from Jessie, seeing Bertha's friends was a duty now. How strange other people were compared to people one knew as he'd known Bertha. Their bodies, their clothes, the things they would or would not do in front of other people, the way they moved, their smell, their emanations.

That he and Jessie, their neighbour of twenty-five years, and his wife's friend from schooldays, should look after each other would have been a sensible solution and was expected and hoped for by friends and family, particularly John, and perhaps by George and Jessie. They were entirely comfortable with each other. He knew, she told George, he only had to mention if he wanted her to see to the house, and he was welcome, as always, to come and eat in hers, but she equally sensed that he'd want to get back on his own feet first after their fairly intense collaboration over funeral arrangements and John's visit. 'It'll give me some occupation, Jess,' he told her, 'keeping the house as she'd have liked it. I need a bit of time on my own not thinking. But don't forget – call on me the minute you need anything done, any job I mean. It'll help to be busy. I'm just not feeling very sociable at present.'

When he was with Bertha's friends it was their Bertha he talked about, that they wanted to think he was loyal to. But it was not that Bertha he wanted to bring back to his consciousness. It was the woman neither Jessie nor the boy knew about, nor her friends or all those who praised her good works. It was a Bertha he sensed even he had not been fully aware of and was just beginning to realise.

One afternoon he had a touch of fever. He stood against a radiator when it was so cold everywhere else his knees ached, and he felt fixed and paralysed. He stood and shuddered and swayed his pelvis and his words became a chant 'Oh God Bertha, Oh God Bertha' over and over. When he could push himself away, instead of going to get ready to go out and help Thompson at the pub, which is what he was meant to be doing, he went straight to the bed and with the help of the bed and bedclothes and his own heat produced a simulacrum for his hand to explore and his thighs to press, but he could not work off his restlessness. He couldn't masturbate without a woman in mind. His bed was not a place he could think of Margaret in and nothing else came. He got up and went uselessly to and fro, putting on the kettle, turning it off, going upstairs again, opening and closing doors, finally to the bathroom, and closed and opened the curtains in one contradictory movement and there the sudden solving of this irritating restlessness lighted up all the sky. It was the moon, the moon who was sending him hither and thither as she dragged the tides to and fro mindlessly. But she herself was not restless. The beautiful calm light lay evenly on all the frosty world and up there was the silver cause of it.

He came in one cold June evening unprepared for the emptiness of the house. He decided to light a fire but he layed it impatiently and the insufficient kindling burnt out before the coal caught. Now it was worse than before with bits of burnt paper floating about. Normally he would have taken it apart, cleaned the grate and built it up properly but the stupidity of his body would not let him stop ruining it when he got a few more sticks alight. He spent a long time fiddling, making it, unmaking it in a mindless almost exaggeratedly clumsy way, something in him gone obstinate, self-mocking, sneering. He felt a sob, a sullen self-pity rising within him and before it could catch him and overwhelm him he stood up, went to the bedroom, levered off both his shoes without undoing the laces, upped his legs and rolled under the coverlet all in one movement without pause, without pause to think, holding his breath against the misery. And there he lay without moving, his forehead and nose pressed into the pillow, his thighs heavy on his hands, pressing his weight into the dark, trying to press out the awful ache of loneliness, to smother the gap of nothingness weakening his limbs, the gap where his wife used to be whose only trace was absence.

He must have slept for at a certain point he realised he was now awake. He heard a car door slam across the street, the people who lived there coming home late, for it was dark now and the rest of the street quiet. He got up, had the meal he had been going to eat by the fire, then washed and went to bed properly, folding his clothes, putting things away, like a man, sober but a bit frail and wobbly, after a hangover.

When the warm weather came his memories materialised. He had begun looking after the house again, doing automatically the things she had done without having to think 'What would Bertha like done now or here?' because they had been so much a part of their life that he knew them without knowing he did. One hot morning he surprised himself drawing the curtain half way across the big picture window in the sitting room. It was a habit he had opposed when he was first back in the house in the mornings. He wanted the room light. He had only been doing these things for something to do, though doubtless he had tried to think of Bertha's actions so he could imagine a 'she' with wishes for him to carry out even if, specially if, he opposed them. It wasn't an image of his hand drawing the curtain that had impelled his muscles. Seeing the strong sunlight making a patch on the sofa-back she always protected, the image had been of her noticing it and her hand and arm reaching up at the same time to send the curtain rattling across casting shade, but of course it had been instantaneous with his movement. It was some time before she was present to him again but as he took on more of her activities so he began to feel the logic of her habits, her attitudes. Doing things he thought she would have liked done, he gradually took on more of her tastes. Since she wasn't there to protect the sofa from fading in the strong light, he would have to be the person who thought of that as well as the one who loved the sunlight.

It was when he found himself regarding himself as she had that she suddenly came back, she was there in his mind thinking his thoughts for him. Coming in absorbed from doing a job he had been enjoying on the car, he kicked off his boots and dirty clothes, leaving them as usual in a heap by the back door, cleaned off the worst in the kitchen sink, laid the tea out and whistled. He was half-way upstairs to get a clean shirt (so he and Bertha could enjoy a civilised tea together) before he realised. He had felt so at peace in the garage tinkering with the car, so relaxed by the feeling of the other person also going about their business in the house, relaxed and refreshed with the anticipation of tea, which Bertha wetted when she heard his signal that he was nearly ready.

'I will just continue on up and lie face downwards on the bed in bitterness and sullenness,' his bones said, 'and I will just lie there and lie there and not get up again.' 'Don't be angry,' he heard Bertha say, 'you know you will have to get up in the end. Why waste this hour you were looking forward to? You can make the tea yourself perfectly well.' And indeed it was a spring evening of poignant fragile delicacy. He continued on up and sat on the bed weeping. 'Bertha, Bertha, I forgot. Oh how selfish. Hold me love, hold me. There, there, you mustn't go, you mustn't go. I'll make the tea,' and so he got back the efficacy of the guardian he had brought into being.

Especially when it was cold he made a nest of warmth at the bottom of the bed with the hot water bottle, the small pink one she used to put at the back of her neck when her arthritis was bad, and the smell of the unused rubber mingled with the womanish smell of an old nighty of hers he'd wrapped round it. He tentatively stretched one foot through the cold sheets down into it, as she used to do, knowing his feet were cold, feeling for the warmth at the top of her thighs. Oh, the delicious soft warmth. He stretched both feet down and dabbled them, then made another patch warm higher up where her hips might have been.

Sometimes when he saw the puzzled reactions of his friends to his absorption in 'things to do at home' or 'got to get back and clean the place up', looking at his watch at seven in the evening, he thought, 'I'm going round the bend.' Then, as he came in through his gate, 'Well, so be it. Why should they mind?' After all, they'd kept saying he should snap out of it, get another woman, be busy, keep company. Well, so he had snapped out of it or rather, Bertha had, as always, helped him to do so. He had wanted to tell at least Margaret who had been so good to him, that he thought he was seeing light at the end of the tunnel. He only had little glimpses of the way to it but he felt if he didn't leave the house too long, if he cultivated these occasions of expectancy, he might secure it. But her look when, making an excuse for not going home with her that night (which he still sometimes did), he said 'I feel I'm expected in the house,' made him change 'Bertha is expecting me' to 'Bertha wouldn't have liked me to neglect it.' It was better not to try and explain to her that it wasn't a memory of Bertha he was living with; it was her presence that comforted him and gave him occupation and pleasure in living.

Interruptions irritated him, even someone coming to the door for a donation for charity or to read the gasmeter which he would formerly have welcomed. Sometimes he was waiting for something. He hadn't time, or rather couldn't concentrate except on what his inner ear was listening for. And yet nobody was coming. He wasn't expecting a phone call. There wasn't anything. Just the habit of expectancy and the emptiness, the restlessness when there was nothing there. Well, he would have to provide, as when coming in for a meal which Bertha used to have laid all ready. These days he had learnt to be both provider and looked to be provided for.

He gave himself high days and holidays like Friday nights in the old days, and mundane workaday weekdays in between. He put clean sheets on the bed, ran the bath, waited as he used to, to give her time, putting everything away clean and tidy downstairs the while, and then in the bathroom from which he emerged clean and gleaming. He got into bed and oh the fresh sheets, the warm washed body faint orris-powdered, the womanish smell of warmed cloth. He snuggled down vigorously. 'Bertha?' he said softly and heard 'George' whispered so near within his arm. Never any question. It was always 'Bertha?' answered by 'George'. He spread her hair, his hand explored from cupped breast flopped against his, he squeezed their nipples together, round the curves into the crevices and heard her little sighs and grunts and almost growly breathing in his own pushing out of voiced breaths.

Come my love, snuggle in under me, let me make you comfortable, oh you're lovely (stroking the shot silk of her skin on her breast) lovely (dabbling with his fingers in the mouth in the moist warmth at the top of thighs). Her thighs had been so soft and plump so rounded to his palm like a breast, a breast and then up to the little lips warm moistening with licked fingers not acrid spurt of liquor. Now. Now Bertha, now Bertha now come on come on come Bertha love, just for you, for you mmm mmm. He seized his left hand with his right, tenderly guiding it as hers to hold his swollen penis, holding it tenderly but firmly then with a fierce grip his larger right hand round both making her hand do so expertly what he needed, guiding it in, ever receptive these nights, ever just right just ready only the one need, the one rhythm to satisfy, his coming absolutely at one with her, no shrinking no halting, her literally his. Oh my Bertha, Bertha this is for you for you, love you, he groaned and shouted and mumbled his need, his exquisite painful pleasure and with a long grunt collapsed in content and satisfaction and rest clasping the warm still body compatible at every point the body that he had brought to warm moist odorous rest.

'You may think I'm off my chump,' he was saying to Thompson during a serious drinking session they had planned about a fortnight before Christmas, 'but it works. It's because the house is empty I want to get back there. At first I just had to get back there to make sure I still could feel she was there. It isn't the past, Scottie, we can't live off the past. She taught me that. You know that. You know that very well.' There were times, like these, when George hoped that with a little more drink Thompson would reveal something of what must have been an eventful personal life, but he never did. His Berth, his complaisant new woman he was beginning to get to know and spend time with, give thought to, encourage and bring out, was not to be found among the remains of her past life, though he hadn't thrown out all her things. She was there where she'd always been for him, in the house, yes, but in him.

Nowadays he realised that something in the atmosphere, almost like a whistle just beyond the range of his hearing when he was with people, was the call of expectancy, not sexual arousal any more. He would follow it, rounding the last corner before their house with rising excitement and happiness, to enjoy the state for its own sake now, for it led to nothing but its waning, then morning again, a bit like those trick drawings of staircases, strange tricks of perspective.

He often spent a happy evening pottering around in his house and garage, which looked after him, he told people, because he looked after it. He was putting off the delicious moment when he would get into bed that she had made all warm and smelling of her. He realised that the moment he was putting off was also when he should find it, the moment, empty. So he got to enjoying the anticipation which gave life to his hours as oxygen does to blood, and went tired and content to his bed to sleep. Just as sometimes in normal life together each will find a day, a night, on their own without confidences, without explaining, without looking for a response, the greatest luxury and rest, so he was sometimes relieved that he didn't always have to create excitement.

He went round to fix a co-CAB worker's mower one Saturday afternoon. The wife invited him to stay for supper but, seeing an awkward look fleet across his face the man thought he shouldn't have presumed that George had nothing to do. 'Expected home?' he provided tactfully. 'Yes,' George said. 'Another time I'd like to, thank you very much, but I'd better be getting back now. Got someone coming. I've got quite a bit to do before the light goes. That motor should be all right now, should see you through this season anyway. Let me know if you have any more trouble with it.'

'Yes,' he thought as he waved to the man, 'that's right. I am expected. I expect me. I'm expecting my evening at home.' He hummed to himself as he walked home and when he'd let himself in and shut the door paused in the hall, appreciating that it had all been tidied so it was 'nice to come into' and the plant on the dusted hall stand fresh and watered. He washed his hands in the kitchen, put on the kettle, laid the table and, making for the stairs to go and change his shirt, gave a joyful little whistle.

Chair

Coming down in the night to get some water I do not wish to disturb the breath of the dark by turning on the light. The house was warm and peaceful. I went back to my room as if from sitting in the dark by someone sleeping, sleeping well, breathing regularly with no sound.

It is very quiet in the house, very still. There is no one to see the chair in the hall, but it stands there as the slight thinning of the night before summer dawn begins its outline, begins to define it out of the block of the dark
as a painter, by brushing in a focus on space, might make emerge bar back, plane of wood, dimension where a person may sit

so all we can do to recognise the object is to listen to the air at the point where it laps it, listen to the waves of light beating up against bar back, slender frame, wooden seat. As the light breathes stronger, separating the chair from the dusk in the hall, it moves out into definition against the white wall;

the chair is placed, poised, by the light. It holds in its shadowed seat all who have sat there, all those who may come.

Cup full of shadows

A cup empty, it may be no use to you when you are thirsty, in from a long walk, knives in the throat from dryness, an empty cup no use under the tyranny of practical need

but that cup there now, clean on a clean wiped saucer, no mess of crumbs around, no smears or gathered pattern of skin of cold milk tea, suggesting tea drunk, that someone had been,
that cup there now empty could have anything in.

You can see the hand, brown from the sun, wrinkled from work, tilting the jug to pour cool dense milk. A pretty jug, brought from Italy. The hot steam of thin tea likewise, unclogging the pores, loosening the coagulation of phlegm, steam of tea on the black window of a winter kitchen morning. At the same time a cup of cocoa with milk froth on it and a spoon stirring in plenty of sugar to be carried upstairs for the child in bed, come home with fever early a spring afternoon, cup placed on tray in case, in the restlessness of its fever, it turns it over. Or empty clean white cup among others set for breakfast, late at night in the room, left ready for the morning, the clock audible in the waiting hours, the room at last eased out into all the space between now and morning, for nothing will come in but these hours to itself, nothing between this point of rest from occupation and the time when they will all be down, getting breakfast down and off to work. One stands tipping the cup to the lips while eyes and other hand flick through papers, smooth hair. Used cup is downed with a clatter far from saucer, arms legs head body off through the door.

There are all those things now. Once fill it with tea, sit down to drink it and alternatives are gone. The cup's potential has gone. It holds nothing

whereas a cup of shadows is filled with possibilities.

Chasing drops of water

He jumped violently as his father's voice penetrated and amplified within the steamy seclusion of the bathroom: 'Get out of that bath, Alan, and get to bed. You must have been in there at least an hour.' 'Coming, Dad,' he managed but his low murmur would not have reached the door let alone outside it, down the passage and down the stairs his father was shouting up.

He realised he'd been cold for some time. The water was barely tepid.

He'd started with two drips. He always started off vowing to leave them alone to race each other, once he'd splashed the water high up on the side of the bath to start them off, and do the best of three, and get out of the bath then and there, but he could never resist helping on one or the other, sometimes the one that seemed to be stuck, sometimes the one nearest the surface of the bathwater so he could get some result, impatient to start again. Sometimes the drops of water he fluttered from his fingers missed the sliding globes and made a third contending drip, or a trickle that provided a slanting route, a runnel of water that if he could get one of his drips into he knew would take it at once to the end of its course, and come out by his knee, like if you landed on a long snake playing snakes and ladders and at once went diagonally a long way fast – only down was winning for the drops of water, not losing.

But what had detained him so long this evening, apart from being very tired but too young to realise that it was tiredness that was preventing him from getting to bed, was that he had realised a dilemma. He'd realised why, whichever one reached the water first he couldn't leave it at that but wanted to start again; and why even when he'd made a delta of trickles, with his dripping finger-tips, getting the streams to divide, to multiply, to swallow drops and runnels lower down, to overtake tributaries, there was never a real finish. To force himself out of the bath, dry and get to bed was always cutting something off, ending it without it being finished. It was because if it went one way it couldn't go another way. He wanted to see which way it would go on its own; but he couldn't resist the interest of introducing alternatives, of wanting to see what would happen if he added more water from on top.

'Alan,' his father roared. In desperation the boy splashed a handful of water at the side of the bath obliterating the drips he'd started for a 'final run' but starting many more, pulled the plug out and ran into his bedroom, moist and shivering in his towel. 'I'm in bed, Dad,' he called loudly as he gave a quick rub and pulled on his pyjamas which stuck on his damp flesh.

'About time too,' his Dad said puffing in. 'Another time you take so long I won't come up. I've got things to do you know. You should have been asleep by now. And who didn't dry their feet?' noticing the print marks on the floor. 'I suppose you've left it to me or your Mum to clear up the swamp in the bathroom.' The boy made to get out of bed to go and do it. 'No, no. You stay put now you are there, but you've got to stop this dreaming in the bath and get to bed earlier.'

Alan felt relieved at his father's launching on this long-winded type of grumbling for it meant that it was OK, that he was going to look at a book with him, or tell him something, and run his hand through his hair and straighten his bed and tuck him up and say 'Nighty-night, Sleepy-tight, Mind the fleas don't bitey-bite.' Indeed he'd got one of Alan's football annuals tucked under his arm. The boy wanted to explain why he'd been so long in the bath, he hadn't fallen asleep and he wasn't taking no notice of what he'd been told. 'Dad,' he said, this time really on the verge of sleep, while his father was reading from the book. 'Alan, this is interesting. I thought this one was your favourite. Now, I was at that game and it really was something. Oh, you're tired. Well tomorrow then.' 'No, Dad. I do like you reading to me but I've just seen, when I was in the bath I saw...' It had gone. Explaining it to his Dad made it sound different, ordinary, stupid. His Dad, though, having been disappointed of his ritual usually so appreciated by his son, was waiting. 'Well, what, sleepy head? You know I think you did fall asleep in that bath. Got to watch that you know. What did you see – a dinosaur coming up out of the plug-hole?'

'No, it's that if it goes one way it can't go another way.' His father's affectionate chant about the fleas came strange and mag-nified through his sleep-filled head.

Ant nest

As the establishment of an ant citadel under the top-soil makes desert a considerable area which yet shows a green surface, extending the sterility of the soil by the continuance of multifarious activity below, concentrated, unremitting, absorbing, unseen,

resulting in a lack of hold in such plants as go on attempting to grow on the soil, for they have to survive with a very curtailed rooting system – the honeycombed areas retain no moisture and have no nourishment –

So the death of his child years ago, unknown to most of his acquaintance, a wound covered over with courage, and determination to continue alive in this world, laid beneath layers of activity – the walking tours with his brother, the visits, in spring and autumn usually, to his wife's parents on the Welsh borders, the bringing of their skiff in off the river for the winter, the fruit-picking at the farm in the Vale of Evesham for his wife to make jam, the sending off for tickets for when the National Companies came to Worcester,

apparent coverage as bright and solid as a full herbaceous border,

So this grief chawing away made a place riddled with holes beneath all the associations, all his filling of his days. When he cracked up in the office over something that would not have worried a junior his colleagues emphasised their disbelief by repeating how perfectly well he had been and normal and competent, with no sign even in the previous day or two that anything was worrying him, but anyone who knew about soil conditions and the ravages a colony of termites makes on substance if left undisturbed would have recognised the ashen skin and lethargy of the man as consequential. The unseeing stare, foredone; closure; concluded;

For there was no body to it, no nourishment to be had from it, all used up and made useless by the life of emasculation perpetually at work below the surface, taking all good from it, preventing conditions of soil recovery whatever was manfully done on the surface up in the air by a few tenacious plants.

Dream

He woke in absolute terror from a dream; and remained rigid for some time with heart banging up into his skull, still constricted with fear. Even as in the dream something at the edge of consciousness suggested that if he stirred, faced the people crowding round, pushed them away, declared 'nonsense', he could have escaped from the nightmare. If he had struck out with a fist or a sharp word, a clean breath of air would have rent the coagulating fog. But it was the fear that kept him in their power, paralysed. The reality clung though physically he knew where his body was, that there was no one else in his house, at least not round his bed where he lay, that the mob, Louise's associates, had not sprawled all over and taken his things. It was the 8.20 a.m. not the 6.30 p.m. bus he had to catch. The half hour left to catch it was seeping away, they were maliciously taking up his time with petty demands, drawing him into attempting to satisfy them, like scratchy children, even though more and more fruitlessly – for of course they didn't care – he was telling them, 'I've got a bus to catch, I've got to leave to catch the 6.30.' No, that was the dream. He hadn't missed the bus yet. That was something. And if the bus was different could it be that they were not waiting for him downstairs, round the fire they had made of his furniture in the middle of the empty stone floor which was his sitting room? He felt cold at the image of his stripped house. His hands and feet were leaden cold. How could he get warm without fabric, without carpet, without chairs to sit in? But he had not missed the bus after all.

At last he stretched a limb, turned, reached out to put on the light. At least let him face the cold, the malign eyes that might be staring at him, the dirty bodies jostling. They were not there. Oh thanks be. But as well not to have moved straight away. The body knew. Lifting very heavy bags yesterday, being unnecessarily heroic to shoulder an acquaintance's load (showing off. If only he had shouldered not heaved) he must have strained something. The soul's fear had been the body's warning. And the mind knew. The dream was the day. It had been real, that mobbing, that closing in. He was there to be fleeced, extirpated from the society he had thought to be part of. Louise was not a thief, nor running a racket, coy front for the bully boys. Her stories of the gypsies were probably made up to glamorise ordinary failure, ordinary petty criminal life, cadging, extortion of a small personal sort, way-ins rather than break-ins. But she'd been out to get him all right, as in the dream, to destroy, dog-in-the-manger, what she had no use for, and she had used her power of malignity and sent her pack of destroyers into his limbs and his gut, poison into his dream from the grove that fringes the slime of the stagnant pool. And the body had produced the lineaments of those people and that frightful evening in his place as you could say that the flinching muscle produces the image of the fist smashing on to the cheek-bone just in time, sometimes, to avoid it.

The sun fallen in fog

Everything outside was coated with black oozings. It was not raining now but the air was dark and low and weeping and the roads and pavements as if sweating black paste. Collars up heads down and suddenly there in the messy gutter a ball like the sun. The only light there was came from its thick oily surface, a bilious yellow dirt-smeared plastic punctured ellipse as if the sun, the only sun there is, had dropped, diminished, finishing here, no strength now to burn or ruin, only gravitational pull of its own ruination, only stopped from being pulled in, pulled down, by the tarmacked surface where it lay in mucky leaves and sodden pulp of litter; still powerful to stir the gut by pulling the strings of the eye to it, lurid nauseous yellow of oily plastic, immobilised, emptied by the punch in its concaved side, no zest to push it out to a buoyancy again.

The sun reduced and lurid, the people hulking through the mist then seemed apocalyptic, demons or saving angels, traitors, sadists, dream-haunting parts of faces glimpsed at crossways; or heaven-sent messengers, heaven sending, bringing a canopy, one at each corner, immanent of bursting into a song, upraising soul-bearers, their breath, if they were to get near, balm to hurt skin.

For at such times with the air thin we live on an edge, the strings of the eyes that connect with the gut (which some say is the seat of the soul) twang in the strange light. Every form, every object is dire, important, a flake of the essence;
or shadows only, null, void, nothing.

And up at the height of our faces where we breathe the air that is rarified, dazzling with droplets of obscurity,
we are walking above the surface of the earth

or, seeing again the broken toy for what it is, inert in the gutter, we are wading as deep beneath.

Scream of the kettle

The morning was very quiet. It was a muffled day, the sort that never opens. At eleven it was the same as at seven. No one had come no one had gone. The quiet was like soft cloth round a tired body. Such chocks and sounds of movement and work as went on down the street, in the village, across the fields, were kept outside the perimeter of the still pool by the windless wet and the dark. All that filtered through was that the flotation of the world, the shocks of noise, the disruptions, were things that happened elsewhere.

On the kitchen window-sill against the milk-white that was the air beyond the pane but not connected to it for all was shut and elsewhere, pulsed the red of a geranium, one flowerhead only that had continued after the rest of the flower had died down, as if it too had lost all sense of time, morning or afternoon, day or night, thrusting spring or subsiding autumn.

A piercing scream cut across this atmosphere where the hours passed drop by drop with no rustle, the scream of the kettle boiling.

She had gone to work. She had been careful over cleaning her shoes, seeing that stockings, jacket buttons, gloves were in order. She spent time and care more than necessary to sew back a thread from a loose seam in her glove. She combed her hair a little forward without acknowledging that she was thus covering her inflamed cheek-bone. As she cleaned up every trace of the night's commotion she wiped from her mind any cognisance that anything had happened and spent all her attention on laying together two lines of thread, on pressing flat a collar, on the angle of her hat. At work she was very busy devising a new filing system and doing over fair copies of memos she normally scribbled on a pad. A new ribbon took a long time to put in, and to wash the ink off her hands and re-do her nails longer. She had not time for chat over coffee. In the lunch-hour she went to look something up in the library. What a successful day she had had; how busy, how efficient, how full of competence and activity were her days. She got back to her nicely-ordered flat feeling she was managing very well – draining-board shining clear, fresh boiled wrung dish-cloth on edge of sink, food ready in oven, washing rolled ready to iron, stores in rows in cupboard, cleaning materials (with spares) away on a shelf. She would even be able to do something this evening. She was not as deadbeat as she had expected to be. She could cut out, as planned, the pattern for the dress she was going to make.

Although her supper was ready she wasn't hungry. There was nothing that caught her eye in the evening paper which she usually sat down with over a pot of tea when she got in. She went to the bedroom cupboard to get the material from the shelf there. The white inside of that half of the cupboard which his clothes had darkened forced itself on her eye. Her breath got caught up in its intake and, struggling for it, she let fall her head, face forward blowing into the fur, on to her best coat that hung there. It swung in the space where it had previously been packed in with his clothes, and gravity took her further to the corner of the cupboard, dark, still, soundless once the hangers stopped rattling. She stayed there in a bundle, comfortable where she had fallen, pressed into the fur. Then into that stillness, from within her body into her head though no sound came from her throat, rose a great wail, as if from the far side of the town when it sleeps at night a siren had suddenly broken the air and suffused every street with roll on roll of the echoing sound up to the fourth floor windows.

After the scream came rising and bubbling the noise of sobbing. She cried and cried with a fresh start when she thought of her poor head where he had banged it against the door, and it was throbbing now with each pressure of breath and the skin of her face sore with the salt. Then she stopped and lay pressed into the dark corner of the cupboard for twelve hours, and the silence came back round her like white air pressing up against a window pane and sealing it in from all movement in the world outside.

Up into the trees

The figure went up the track from the valley as if impelled only physically, with the intent but unconnected movement of mesmerism, as when the head is turned to look at something but the feet go on; for there had been a shock. To the whole being. In simple language, as if haltingly, by a brain down to a single strand, words seemed to come, from outside, from a time elsewhere:

How very beautiful the hillside was. The air so sweet. The flaming tree without movement in the cliff of trees; sitting within its glow as under a lampshade so that somehow the colours and the stillness were as if the last breath was held, but without strain. It would be natural, simple, to breathe out and not breathe in again. To go down, in hardly a suspiration, releasing oneself out through the air which was of course composed of all these unglaring glows, as a leaf between one minute and the next detaches itself – Or no, for that implies effort decision volition – finds itself detached, and then is merely in another position. It is in its last resting position. Nothing more is required. On the ground. Hidden. Among the trees its passing is not noticed. Its acceptance as part of the ground is unmarked.

Marigold and green

It is as if someone should say 'marigold' in a foreign language to someone who has never seen that flower. They know the meaning but that dash of orange-gold from the wayside patch does not fill their sight, no gay brave daisy-eye wakes their attention through the dun ground-mist of November.

The person who is ill looks from the window on to the grass. It is not colourless as, against the green carpet of a greengrocer's laid-on stuff, one might make the comparison of strength of colour. It is without colour as it might be nothing. The green is there. You say, 'that is green', but it might as well be blue or orange for all you feel it is real grass, might as well be the blue or orange of the colour television that shifts its acid splashes. Like a bad transfer what you see is that it is fixed on, not what it is. 'Green,' you say. 'It is thick and healthy growing grass, the right colour for grass. I can see that is grass and that it is green.' You can still say that but there is a gap, a separation, a no-man's land between the word-forming head, between the noticing eyes and the knowledge of green. No currents, no connection carries the liveliness across the airless gap to revivify, to nourish, to make operative the feeling of green.

Rapture

A death, a grave illness or even some extraordinary happiness isolates people, wrapping them away from the daily chaffering which deals with the more encompassable middle range of social activities – the cheery 'How are you?' thrown bonhomously across the road at an acquaintance seen after weeks of elsewhere is nonplussed, has no continuation to the truthful answer, 'Bad', and hastens on with no more words

as an exceptional wave might carry a bather, high up in the curve of its roll and lob one up above the tideline

so the joy of Caroline's return to him and the crash some years later of the coach taking their daughter's class on a school outing wrapt him to the same sphere

unreached by voices or eye beams of distant figures marionette-like, silent going here and there away at a tangent the other side of the thick glass

the thickening partition at one time all shot with irridescence and sparkle and flowing with energising air and the other, imprisoning concave walls clad with clinging layers of lack of light

the dank fog in which he was choking

'How are you?' concerned kind people said and, lodged inert behind the jags of the rocks at the foot of the precipice where the huge wave had rolled him, no breathing moving his broken body

'Not too bad,' he said managing some reflex round his mouth and eyes as he got his key into the lock of his door, somehow turned it and got himself inside it.

Calling ships at sea

There are several ways of calling a ship at sea, the telephone directory tells us.

Instead of area codes there are ocean region codes (a slip of the finger on the dial and you'd get the Pacific instead of Atlantic Ocean [east]). You'd need of course to know the ship's name and give the name of the coast radio station, if known. (How one could give it if not known I'm not sure but then I sometimes find the simplest official instructions baffling if you read them carefully.)

If your ship has satellite communications you can even dial direct if the exchange you're dialling from has digital metering. Imagine dialling and hearing it ringing, ringing in all that waste of waters, the dark wave blotting out the cloud-covered sky for hundreds and hundreds of miles and the shrill of a telephone, a muffled trilling in a cupboard among floating spars. Of course you'd need to know the identification number of this ship all at sea that you are wanting to call.

There is even a way of finding out its ocean region code if you don't know it, but for that to be of much use I suppose one would need to know which ocean the ship, listing dangerously, its ballast shifted, fuel tank holed, low down in the water out of control before the storm, was in. Looking under Inmarsat will tell you the ocean code (Atlantic Ocean, west − 874, Indian Ocean − 873, Pacific − 872), but not the ocean, not warn you of that great mass of water filling the horizon, its currents, its rocks, its furies.

Oh ship all at sea, engine fouled, broken-backed, the long rollers running from the horizon pouring through your hold on their remorseless momentum across the world, if I had, never mind what equipment, it is as unlikely you would hear me as when I stand on a cliff and call into the wind. And if you heard, what could that do for you, driven to jagged straits by the inexorable south-easter, into the suck, strong as death, of the coiling currents?

> To direct dial your Inmarsat calls:
> 010
> followed by Ocean region code
> followed by ship's identification no.

Yet I climb to the cliff-top and I call. Who knows but that somewhere in the shriek of the storm sawing through the steel shrouds, in some vibration from the ocean's pounding you may not imagine you hear the tones of a voice?

Two polished chestnuts

The chestnuts in the mud of the ditch looked valuable objects, like old polished desk fitments, so you had to pick them up, to save them, to cherish them.

Colour is determined by the eye (a decision in the brain) but this light that shines at you as if speaking to you from the polished flank seems reflected from deep within. The rich polish is deep laid in the solid piece in your palm, as the gleam of good hair comes from health at source. And then they lie dull on the mantelpiece. Dusty then wrinkled. Getting nasty. The fish whose gleam, whose flash whose quick flick of colour along its back (its taut belly paler) led us on, ever escaping, ever alive, cool and lustreful, lies flaccid on the grit stone of the quay. Unappetising, eye glazed, dimming, stinking.

Some years later (lifetimes if you computed by the different circumstances each had worked their way through in the interval) they were at the same time in the same place – a fête in aid of the local hospital. He still sported, if not the style that had been for the young when she had met him, yet a style for the young of some fashion past. He had not been young then, when they had met, though she had been. She must then, she thought, have seemed like one of this current batch of faithful-dog hangers-on wanting to be the one most useful to his major-domo-ing of the occasion. It hadn't been Friends of the Hospital then but something on the fringes of the political, organising a placard-carrying event in the campaign to unionise the catering trade at the restaurant where she had been working. She must have lost three jobs in the feverish two months she'd had to do with him. How forgotten that time!

It was easy for her to avoid him. He was very taken up with the setting-up of a first aid demonstration in the marquee. How could I ever have touched him, she thought, glancing to confirm that it really was him but anxious lest her look should alert his. She had not been particularly satisfied with life earlier that day and was now extremely glad to be her, she who had been his acolyte, who had wanted so much to be a part of anything, everything he did that she would have swapped skins. Incredible! She put an extra pound in the collecting box at the gate as she went out in expiation of the disloyalty she felt, not to him, for she had

159

done more than keep her word long after she knew him to be chaff, but to her own past self, and in gratitude for her own life far away from all that now.

The owner of the holiday house was having a clear-out getting the house ready for the next let. Those mouldy lumps on the mantelpiece, old conkers were they, picked up on some walk? People didn't seem able to go a walk without bringing things back from the woods, or if they visited the village, fish from the quay for her to cook or plants to be looked after. She swept them off with other accumulated rubbish on to the fire she'd lit to clear the grate. They flamed with a dim blue lick of fire and glowed dully into crumbles of ash like two fragments of coal, giving off a small warmth.

Extended simile

As when in a tree, the centre having been struck with some dis-
ease the crest flourishes among the crowns of the forest,
nourished through its surface and kept straight in storms
even, by the surrounding growth, yet seeming green and
sappy will one calm day crash its length in ruin making
a trenched gash on the clad hillside;

as when a rock face, solid slab from eternity, weathered, weather-
ing, formed mainly of one substance but with a rift of
softer material lime in granite say, concealed in its core,
splits and crumbles away, tumbling through the air that
has teased out its fault;

as when tree root bursts up flaking the splitting rock it grew from,
each other's downfall, to shrivel in the light, to pulverise
to loose shards,

so 'Why didn't you ask me what sort I wanted?' she says.
'You knew I'd be in soon but of course you can't wait a
minute once you feel like doing something, though it
doesn't matter how long we hang about for you.' 'I thought
I could save a job and get it for you.' 'You ought to know
by now it's just going to give me extra to do because it'll
be me that goes and changes it. I could've got it myself
in the first place with less bother';

so 'I'll not hurry home,' he thought, 'I can pretend I forgot
it was her evening at the clinic. The times I've hurried
and nothing's been ready. Only let myself in for some

work. If I get in at the last moment she'll have seen to the children and she'll just have to shoot out and there won't be time for talk';

so she scrapped and scraped and snapped the new man who would have been kind;

so he crumbled and slid down, no hold for what could have grown again sheltered in surety;

so an avalanche down the dry cliffside, no foothold in scree of shale, the gash of their ruin seen far across the valley

harmed by an old hurt
leaning on a central flaw

cause;
agent;
effect.

The Bermuda Triangle

You are going smoothly and merrily along the roads and the engine starts to buck. There is a feeling of drift in the steering, as when you are caught in crosswinds. There is a gap between driver's hands and wheels which intrudes, takes over, as when a bulky vehicle masks you on one side, breathing heat and disorder, taking your balance of air. A pen going smoothly marking the paper crosses a patch of grease and nothing comes out, the pen slides. Is the car sliding? We are not in touch, not in control, and the car was going so well.

We are swimming in the sunny sea and then, no cloud above or towering cliff to cast shadow, we are labouring in dark water, drawn to the colourless patch outside the cave's mouth. How cold. No dimming: suddenly – bmph! So, skimming evenly, strongly over the lake, a stretch of water that sparkles over to the green sward-like opposite bank, thinking of not much except enjoying your skilfulness, feeling healthy, right, good at it, one oar catches a crab and looking around you realise you are among reed and silt, lurching and ducking through beslimed dead branches overhead. The slow but regular circular movement of a scummy surface takes you with its sweep. You have touched the edge of its down-ward-dragging current. It is unhurried, automatic and will draw you to the centre of its stifling fluid. We set out for the treat, a holiday day, called on friends, sociable and merry. 'No, come on, we've got food, a surprise for you, come on, all arranged.' We waved the basket, neck of bottle showing out of napkin, other drink for the children, packets, cartons, fruit, good things. They joined us, used their day on this, responded – and we found our-selves in a tunnel as in the dream where we are so intently taken away from – carried away from, drifted away from – the very intent we had fixed on. The patch of air, the slimy race, the dark rock face, the opposite direction – it is so near to the road we were on. That air mingles with our air, the tunnel is not in another soil a county away. It is beneath and alongside the path we were going. We come to with the sound of the barrier to the disused canal clashing in our faces. There was no way through after all. It was not open. We cannot get back to the sweet strong daylight, open water, the balanced air, the engine running just right under our hands. We are where we shouldn't be.

The Bermuda Islands are a group in the North Atlantic covering an area of about nineteen square miles. They can be found in the Gazetteer. There is an important naval station there, it says. They grow early vegetables for New York.

At the time when their population was about 20,000 (Capital: Hamilton 2,600) it was further set down that 'the Bermudas are about 600 miles from the coast of the United States and 800 miles north of the West Indies'. Really they are in the open Atlantic and as they have a fine climate and pleasant scenery with luxuriant veg-etation they are much visited by holiday-makers, chiefly Americans. Originally they were colonised in 1609 by a party of English emi-grants shipwrecked on their way to Virginia. 'Bermuda is an im-portant naval base and dockyard. The chief town is Hamilton with two or three thousand people. Their chief products are of the market-gardening kind – potatoes, onions and other vegetables with flowers for table decorations and a large part of the trade is with New York…but modern competition has made their prospects doubtful and at times very dark. Still, the soil is prolific, and these sunny lands living preferably in a languorous ease, should be able to adapt their advantages to the needs of modern life.'

And the poet says:

> Where the remote Bermudas ride
> In the Ocean's bosom unespyed
> From a small boat that rowed along
> The list'ning Winds received this song
>
> What should we do but sing his praise
> That led us through the watery maze
> Into an isle so long unknown
> And yet far kinder than our own?
>
> …
> He gave us this eternal Spring
> Which here enamells everything
>
> …
> He hangs in shade the orange bright
> Like golden lamps in a green night
> …
> Thus sung they in the English boat
> An holy and a chearful note
> And all the way to guide their chime
> With falling oars they kept the time.

But nowhere in the encyclopaedia or in Marvell is there mention of that strange phenomenon known to those who travel in that area either by boat or high over the treacherous seas by plane. Boats have disappeared, all hands lost, sailing apparently in calm seas. Planes have disappeared or had suddenly to change course and no cause been discovered for such disasters. It is indeed a hurricane area but things have happened there unexplained by any atmospheric change, out of the blue, out of the calm blue. There is nothing in geography to account for the Bermuda Triangle but people know about it.

As a breeze

As a breeze pushes clinging curtains of thick air to show the land that had been there all the while sleeping in sunshine like a brown beast coasting on the water

so sometimes does an idle moment, a moment of slack in our day, let in other times, patches of time which rise from where they lie sleeping, coiled spring, papery dried flower, to open out and suffuse the air of our day

as the land made space for fills our sight.

Earthquake detection

Movements people do not notice as they go about their daily business letting doors slam, revving up cars, banging down boxes, running up and down barging into sideboards, may be registered on the Richter Scale; but a cat will dart up the curtains, snakes tie themselves up into knots, farm animals stamp restlessly when the surface of the world is calm by our measurements.

There is sometimes a flitter in the glass, a flicker as of a signal, in the room, as if whatever lights it had something passed across its eye for a fraction of a second. You realise there has been a mouse when you have just not seen the tip of its tail streaking into the wall; you sense that the cups on the hooks in the kitchen have been swinging only now they are stilled; only when the vibration has passed do you hear the tiny tintabulation:

an alteration in the air pressure, a twitch through the eyelid, minuscule manifestations within the cavern of quiet, out of reach of the most sensitive seismograph. 'My eyes are tired,' we say or 'I've got a lot on my mind, I can't concentrate.' If tadpoles squiggle across they are floaters in the eye;

but the dog takes notice of what we do not recognise we hear, thin metallic warning of whistle from off what great upheavals and shock, what sun spots flailing, what white light of brilliance in the upper air

affecting the cavities in our bones as a passing car ruffles the edge of shadow thrown into a back room.

In the air

As a dog will stop in its head-down busy, hither-thither pursuit of scent, freeze and lift its head, perhaps one paw up in mid-lollop

so we are sometimes taken aback by the thread that perpetually reels on to the bobbin of our day snapping.

The dog has heard a whistle beyond our ken. Because we cannot hear the sound, to us the animal seems magically to smell presences, to whiff happenings

as when the channels of the air are freed by a shift of current for the conveyance of knowledge to us – an apprehension rather, that the atmosphere is altering – and we would do well to take into account changed circumstances, some delivery off-loading, the thread snapping.

The dog halts for the whistle. I will down tools and expect you.

The thread

There was the thread, the thread you see, and she followed it. Curdie, no that was a boy, Curdie and the thread, the good boy, he got her through. Or there was a fall of rock and it was buried, she had to scrabble with her hands and they never got them out those people trapped underneath when the earthquake collapsed the buildings. I can remember the man with his bare hands, they were bare, raw, that's it, skinned – but it must have been a picture of course.

But the thread was there, sometimes – he was losing it, losing his thought.

Yes, that was the way the thread went, it came and went, elusive as thought – now it flashed into focus, now he had it, him sitting reading to his little girl – but he can't have had that book as a child, he hadn't had that sort of childhood.

Thinking about the thread, the idea, myth of the thread was a good way to get you applying yourself, persisting, and he had, hadn't he, he'd gone on searching with his dog in the rubble long after the others had given up.

So that thinking, which he'd thought he'd come to as a solid thing like chipping away shale and muck to get at a bit of core, a thing like a lump of coal, usable, source of energy, so that it didn't matter what you thought, it was a rope ladder to get you across somewhere, get you through the mess, something you pretended, no, not pretended – made up? – to be doing to give a reason for going on. Made up. Ah perhaps something you made, engineered, he'd like it when they called him Monsieur l'Ingenieur, ingenious. Not for a reason – you don't need a reason for going on, you need a road, a way, ah yes a means. A way of going. That was tautology. You could just say 'a way'.

'Tell Alice' (you think I don't know she's dead, he heard his crafty thought within his head and in the same flash behaved as if he didn't), 'keep her fingers on the golden thread.' If it's all a fancy, if there isn't something that's true, then there isn't untrue and you were back where you were. He was getting there, getting down that path and this time he would get there, he could still breathe he could still tell them even though they couldn't move the rock off him.

If there isn't anything that's true, the opposite of true was false. But it couldn't be false because you can't have an opposite to something that doesn't exist. Though what about negative numbers?

Alice was cleverer than he was he should have asked her. But she could never explain things like he could but after all he'd been a teacher. So if no true, no false and nothing true means everything false. Yes, he'd got it. 'Useful,' he said. They bent low pretending they could hear to encourage him to speak some more. Useful. It was all useful. Alice's knitting had been useful. The thread and the rope ladder and the bridge were useful. Useful was much more useful than true.

If he had realised that it was his son who was holding his hand he might have tried to speak in his type of hearty old reprobate he'd put on for years for young people and said something in character like 'Bugger the truth' because he knew they thought he thought truth was the pearl so he had it both ways. They would have been his next, last words but he kept his secret from them till the end because he had got beyond the division of time that living beings need in order to negotiate it, to a point where command question statement implying continuing into a future from the past were neither true, false or useful.

Malaria

'Men have died from time to time, and worms have eaten them, but not for love.'
So said Rosalind, playing her part in *As You Like It*.

On the other hand malaria, the commonest of the tropical diseases, is responsible for some millions of deaths each year.

Morbific exhalations arising from swamps or effluvia from the decomposition of animal or vegetable matter give the disease its name – bad air, bad atmosphere – but what causes it are the animal parasites of the genus *plasmodium* which invade the red corpuscles of the blood. The mosquitoes we fear are merely the carriers which introduce the parasite into the blood.

Medieval medical theorists may not have known much about parasitology or the circulation of the blood but they knew about the affliction of love, the 'loveres maladye of Hereos'. Through an imbalance of the melancholic humour, a lack of moisture in the system, part of the head is affected and thus people are made mad by the distemper of love. 'Amor est mentis insania' – love is a disease of the mind and the spirit wanders dolefully through a brain empty of all but sorrow. Although they knew nothing of vaccination their findings were that this sickness unto death could only be cured by whoever had caused it.

She would go along, she thought, she would go along at six, because it was good to have a walk before she settled in for the evening.

A great deal is known about the parasite that causes malaria.

She had fixed her will so strongly on being in a position to pass the shop where he got his cigarettes, at the exact right time, that for the half hour in which she was rushing to get done things whose omission might give a loophole for enquiry, she was almost shaking with unused intent and had no concentration. She went up and down the stairs ten times before she had gathered the clothes to iron, set the iron up, and was ironing a sleeve when she realised it would be better to get the stew to the point where she could leave it while she was out for fifteen minutes.

The plasmodium parasites penetrate the red corpuscles and multiply there. The sporelike bodies they form then enter other cells.

The looks they would exchange when she was in the newsagents came between her and the sink. Her decision, her absolute intention, to go along had allowed these play acts back into her mind. She was startled to find them still there as complete and as totally occupying the space, as if a three-dimensional cinema screen had lined her brain sealing everything else out, as they had been for that hectic month six years ago. She had not seen or heard of him since then, and had she, with the real solid husband and child she loved filling her thoughts, and the job that was not bad and brought in some money and friends, considered whether it was safe to think of Tom she would have smiled and felt sure the nerve he had been so adept at twanging, the gut even the thought of hearing his voice had once turned over, would have no reaction in them; unless perhaps it was slight disdain and perhaps pity, for she had known him for no good in the end. He had cured her with his selfishness and lack of thought for her.

Absorbed in transactions at the newsagents yesterday she had merely heard his name mentioned and his look, his flaring look, and the low murmur of his voice came, from the very particles of the air it seemed, now she was alone in her kitchen, and this mirage put beyond the margin of her consciousness the sound of water running over the clothes, so that it had poured over on to the floor before she realised it. A shirt-sleeve had blocked the overflow hole.

The causes of the particular effects on the human body of this disease lie in the features of the life-cycle of the malarial parasite, which, as I have said, has been much researched.

At a certain stage of malaria, sexual forms of the plasmodium circulate in the blood and when they are ingested into the stomach of the anophelene mosquito (it is the conjunction of this type of mosquito and enough warmth and humidity to allow the parasite to develop in them that provide ideal malarial conditions), the male and female gemetocytes unite, penetrate the stomach wall and form an oocyst. Sporozoites are liberated from this in from one to three weeks (again according to the temperature). They find their way to the salivary glands and from there into the bloodstream of man. Once present in the human liver cells, merozoites are liberated after eight and a half days and they take a ride on the circulating red blood corpuscles from which they may enter new liver cells (though not *P. Falciparum*).* Here they may lie dormant for many months and it is probably this that accounts for the recurrence of benignant tertian and quartan fevers, possible months or even years after the first infection.

In the red cell the merozoite develops first into a ring form, then by asexual reproduction into a schizont from which a new batch of merozoites are liberated into the blood when the red cell is ruptured. This asexual reproduction takes forty-eight hours in the Tertian malarias and seventy-two hours in Quartan malaria accounting for the interval between the rigors and fevers in those cases, for they occur when the new shower of merozoites enters the blood. Each merozoite enters a new red cell and several cycles of schizogony usually occur before some merozoites invading red cells develop not into schizonts but into male and female gametocytes, and this brings round the cycle.

Thus the human sufferer will probably experience something like the following:

For the first few days there is usually either continuous or remittent fever with general malaise, headache, and vomiting but by the end of a week the typical periodicity, with rigors on every alternate or every third day, is often becoming apparent. (It was this that gave rise to the name the disease used to be known by – Tertian Fever.) In relapses, that stage may start at once. In some

---

* NOTE: *Plasmodium falciparum* behaves somewhat differently. It does not lie dormant in the liver cells. Falciparum malaria is much more likely to be fatal and is called 'pernicious' or 'malignant' because clumps of plasmodium falciparum may block capillaries in the vital organs – brain and spinal nervous system and the lungs, at any time during the course of the disease and so act with a swiftness (pernicity) not usual with other strains, which are only 'injurious' or capable of doing harm.

patients no regular pattern ever emerges, probably because they harbour two or more 'families' of parasites at different stages of development. As is generally known, the typical attack of malaria starts with a cold stage with shivering or *rigors* which can last from a few minutes to a couple of hours, followed by a hot stage with a severe headache, vomiting, a hot dry skin and high fever. Finally profuse sweating for an hour or two brings down the temperature, and the patient feels better, possibly remaining so until the next attack two or three days later.

The reason for the characteristic alternation of chills, fever and sweating that anyone attacked by malaria suffers is that with the dissolution of the corpuscles of the blood the products of the parasite are freed into the plasma.

Now she knew she was going to see him, had decided what she would do – she would buy some matches and a bar of chocolate for a treat after Jody's tea – she was calmer. It didn't seem to matter so frantically that she get there now, since she intended to see him and this somehow made her feel there was understanding between them. With this loosening of the knot of anxiety happiness enabled her to get her work done well.

Having bought her matches and taken her time over the choosing of a bar of chocolate she couldn't delay much longer at the shop. The newsagent, used to her being in a rush, never one to linger and chat though pleasant enough, asked her, 'No Jody today then?' 'His Granny collects him from nursery on Tuesdays and gives him and Sheba a bit of a run in the park.' 'Gives you a bit of a break then.' 'Yes,' she said, 'it is a help, and the longer evenings help too, don't they?' She must have missed him. The shop was empty except for an untidy old woman with a sheaf of papers at the copying machine. He was as absent from her world as when she knew he was away and would never get in touch with her. How even more ridiculous she would seem trying to introduce lightly some remark that could lead to her mentioning his name. The last thing he'd want was to hear that someone had been asking for him, and the last thing she wanted that anyone should notice her interest. 'But goodness, how quickly the time goes – they'll be back any minute expecting their tea.' This would give some justification to her looking rather often through the door up the road while she was talking. The newsagent had to call her back for her to pick up from the counter her change and the paper bag with her two purchases in.

Well, now she could concentrate on Susan, her mother-in-law, and Jody and tea, and get the ironing done, and enjoy the evening without the distraction of missing her one chance with Tom. If she had met him he might have wanted to arrange to see her that evening – or nothing (though when, she reminded herself, had he ever made or stuck to an arrangement or taken into account the difficulties she had to overcome to make time available?). It had only ever been when she'd happened to be there, met by chance, that he'd wanted her. He had only ever made things more difficult for her. It was a good thing she knew what he was like. She didn't regret spending her afternoon on trying, but now that had lanced her curiosity. The fear of being made ridiculous stifled her desire, and she was well rid of interest in him, and much the better for that. He was impossible, impossible; but how she longed for him not to be.

As we have seen the cause of malaria has been pin-pointed and (brought up to believe there is a tangible thread leading from cause to effect if we can find it – find it and break it) we would therefore presume that the cause once known, the disease could be wiped out. Much of course can, and has been, done.

Some measures aim at the sources. We can prevent the breeding of anophelene mosquitoes, which means draining all swamps, marshes and treating standing water. If you think how impossible even in a tiny part of the earth the size of England it would be to catch up with and deal with puddles of spilt oil in yards, say, or caches of accumulated litter, behind rocks, in dells, round dustbins, lining walls in disused premises behind padlocked rotting gates, then imagine 'treating the standing water' in the world. My informant rightly points out that 'there are some places in the world where the task is nearly impossible'. But we must add that there are many places where efforts to stamp out malaria are proving successful.

Apart from that we can, of course, try to avoid getting bitten by the fly. There is wire-meshing. Day or night, every minute of every day and night if you live in an infested area and have fixed wire meshing over all apertures to your house, you must never relax your vigilance. One careless visitor who does not latch the screen door and which a puff of air or the nose of a dog pushes ajar, one child running out to fetch something and 'coming back in a minute', will start up the cycle again.

In order not to be bitten without knowing it – asleep – by a mosquito that may have evaded these guards, you can make sure that the mosquito net shrouding your bed has not the slightest rent, the tiniest rip, that no toe of restless child ever slips down in sleep to trail on the floor at the edge of the net, that the arm flung from dream does not break through the defences.

You can also cover your skin entirely, if you do go out from the fortress of your dwelling – long sleeves closed at the wrists, tight up round the neck, no access down to the ankles. Some even apply a repellant lotion to those parts of the body it is not possible to bury entirely.

There is the spraying of DDT which has had great effect in the past but begins to be doubted as the cure-all it was believed to be when first introduced.

But because malaria is an infectious disease another line of attack has concentrated not on elimination but on restricting its spread. Although the term 'infectious disease' might logically be applied to any illness which results from invasion of the body by a micro-organism, our use of the term usually refers to diseases which spread by direct contact between people, and the way to prevent this spread is, of course, by isolating those infected.

With some fevers, although the symptoms seem analogous to those of malaria, and although quite a bit of detailed observation as to the prevalence, development, spread and progress of the disease has been recorded, there is not the same possibility of getting to grips with it. For one thing where there is no consensus of the will to do so, there will be no concerted joining of efforts, a very necessary prerequisite for the control of *contagious* diseases. The struggle is carried on obscurely here and there, backyard science, so to speak, by a few dedicated, convinced but unfashionable souls. They are held back by lack of recognition, lack of resources at their disposal and this in its turn limits the opportunities to apply such findings as they have carefully assembled over periods of time

but the chief obstacle to their having much effect lies in their prescription of what is in our societies these days an unnacceptable prophylactic – abstinence, and the cry 'prevention is better than cure', though a popular slogan among those who seek to guide, lay down, and control the ideas behind public policy, is not much more than a pious wish when up against the need to champion the 'individual's right to freedom of choice'. The suggestion, therefore, that patients should practise self-denial in order to protect others from contact with them has sometimes resulted in a righteous outcry against those pragmatists advocating hygienic discipline.

However, with some diseases even were there that common desire and effort to put a co-ordinated nationwide campaign into motion, the results would fall short of complete control. In some diseases only the method of infestation (the carriers) and the symptoms (the behaviour of such organisms as are struck with the disease) have been pinpointed. The vital information needed to extirpate the disease root and branch – the cause itself – eludes us.

'Hallo, old mate. I didn't know you'd returned to this neck of the woods.' Turning from the bar to put his pint down the man just come in joined a younger one whose shirt opened on a sunburnt throat. 'Have a fill-up while I'm still on my feet. Once I sit down I won't be getting up in a hurry. I've been bloody on them since six this morning.'

'Ta. I've been back since Christmas. But I'm living down at Cowcroft now, at my sister's.' As he took a long draught from the fresh pint his smooth skin moved over his Adam's apple. 'I thought I might find Derrick here. Someone said he might have some work at that new centre he's starting up.'

'I haven't seen him in here lately. Has Derrick been in, Stan?' he called to the landlord. 'No, well, you might find him at the Club a bit later. You know, he's taken up with that Thomas woman who used to be his cashier. He was very pally with two of her brothers, and they all use the club.

'Which reminds me of someone I *have* seen. That little stunner Sally Elphidge – Sally Taylor of course she is now. Got a nipper too. Seen her walking her dog of a Sunday morning. In fact I almost bumped into her this evening. Hurrying out of Bailey's she was, as I went in to get me fags and paper. She was wrapped up in her thoughts and she didn't see me, or she'd have spoken to me. She always stops to have a word when I see her in the street, and asks after Mollie. She's got nice manners that one. Lovely girl. And for all she looked a bit worried, what a stunner, eh Tom? I wouldn't mind taking her out for a drink and a walk by the river myself if I wasn't a married man.'

'Go on with you, Jim, whenever did being married stop you from trying it on?' Stan, who was wiping tables nearby said, to save Tom embarrassment. The older man was notorious for his susceptibility and his soft heart and romantic ideas about women, though his devotion to his invalid wife was also known and his friends kept up the banter about his reputation for sexual adventures to cheer him up and comfort him. Tom laughed but as he stood at the bar getting the next drinks the muscles at the back of his neck and his calves tightened, and the fine line of his moustache, just a carefully drawn arc on his upper lip, stiffened as he ordered.

Dennis Taylor was pleased that Sally didn't want to go out for a meal in a restaurant which they did occasionally when they could get a baby-sitter and which he knew she preferred to going down to the pub 'sitting around drinking in a smoky atmosphere spending twice as much as we could get a good meal for, and still hungry when we get home.' In fact it was she who suggested that, as it was a lovely evening, should they just walk down the hill to the Crown? His mother had been with Jody all afternoon and might want to get home reasonably early. Wasn't it the Crown's B team's home match? They needn't stay till closing time, but could come home for supper. She had cooked a casserole ready. 'And we could have an early night,' he said kissing her neck under where she'd put her hair up. She looked very pretty. She squeezed the wandering hand as it was beginning to disarray the blouse she had just put on. '*And* we could have an early night,' she answered with full, knowing bright eyes. 'But not *this* early. Let's go while Jody's happy in the bathroom with Susan.'

Infection and immunity

The result of any infection depends partly on the virulence and number of the invading organisms and partly on the state of the patient's defences against them. The state of his defences depends partly on his natural immunity which may be good or bad according to his race and heredity and may have been reduced by such factors as malnutrition, worry and overwork, and partly on acquired immunity resulting from previous infection or prophylactic innoculation with this particular organism. Such innoculations given to stimulate the formation of antibodies constitute active immunisation and are widely used in the prevention of such diseases as smallpox, diphtheria, tetanus, enteric fever and poliomyelitis. Passive immunisation means conferring temporary protection against a disease by injecting serum containing the specific antibodies; such serum is obtained from humans who have recovered from the disease or from horses actively immunised for this purpose.

Some people after recovering from an infectious disease continue to harbour the specific organisms and may transmit them from time to time to susceptible persons, either by direct contact or by infecting food or water. This carrier state is particularly important in the spread of enteric fever.

Incubation period: this is the time which elapses between the access of organisms to the tissues of a susceptible individual and the onset of the first clinical symptoms. Its duration varies widely in the different infectious diseases but remains fairly constant in each of them.

At the end of the incubation period the infecting organism or its toxic products become distributed throughout the body and give rise to the symptoms and signs of the disease. Common to all infectious diseases are fever, headache, general malaise, loss of appetite, dry furred tongue, hot dry skin and scanty, highly coloured urine; but in addition each has special features.

When Dennis was playing a game of darts (the fixture Sally had remembered was an away game for the A team), and she was admiring the way he sent the dart from the forearm with a delicate flick of the fingers, which pulled his shirt taut against the muscle in his back, and she was feeling glad he was her husband, she caught sight of Jim in the other bar. The toilets were at the back of the bars, and after going through to the Ladies she went into the other bar. She went up to Jim and asked him if she could buy him a drink. 'I didn't know you drank in here, Jim.' 'Well, I don't as a rule.' He was as surprised to see her, and glad. 'I thought you was a mirage, Sal. A heavenly illusion in a thirsty world. Thanks, cheers,' as his full glass was set down. 'Got a night out?' 'Yes, Dennis's Mum's baby-sitting for us. He's in the other bar having a game of darts. But we won't be stopping long. He has such a journey now they've moved him to the Buckley office. But how are things with you? How's Mollie?' 'Oh, so-so, but thank you for asking. Her sister's come over for a few days, so I've got a night out too. If it wasn't for your young Dennis over there, I'd offer to take you dancing. If you was mine I wouldn't bring you to a smoky old hole like this. The young lads these days don't seem to know what to do with their luck when they get it.' 'I'll keep you to that one day, Jim, you'll see, so you better be careful what you promise!' They beamed at each other entirely at ease. 'Actually I suggested we came in here. I know he misses his pub friends and his game of darts. I don't want him to feel swamped by domesticity.' 'Wise girl, Sal,' Jim said then quietly as she turned to go, 'Tom might be along later.' She glanced around the bar as she moved away and raised her voice as she went, to say to Jim 'Give my best to Mollie, Jim. Nice seeing you. Bye for now.'

Dennis came over to the table she was sitting at with another gin and tonic and a packet of crisps. 'You all right for one more game? Then we'll go. It's not too noisy for you is it?' 'I'm fine. You carry on. I've been talking to old Jim Cox. Poor man. Mollie's no better.' He could see she was OK and enjoying being there. 'Oh, I must buy him a drink.' 'I have. You go and play your game.' He was grateful to her for not being an exacting selfish pert little wife like Derrick's, the man he was playing darts with. 'You're a peach,' he said.

Before they left she went to the toilet again. As they set off up the hill, their progress a little impeded by their doing a sort of three-legged race with their arms round each other, she noticed a group of three young men at the corner on the opposite side, one astride a huge motor-cycle. She straightened up a bit and as she recognised Tom took her arm from around Dennis's hips to get a handkerchief from her pocket and didn't put it back. She groaned to herself, 'Oh why now, why now?' He was the one who had taken off his motor-cycle helmet. As she put her handkerchief back in her pocket she snatched off one of her earrings wrapped it in the handkerchief and held that in her fist in her pocket. She felt a surge of queasiness from the one too many gins she'd downed too quickly because they had suddenly wanted to be out of the pub and on their way home. Although the hill was getting steeper at this point they were quickly going away at a tangent from the motor-cycle huddle. 'Goodnight,' she called out and Dennis echoed her greeting, presuming they were people he knew. 'Oh, hi there, Den, goodnight,' Tom answered, looking only at Dennis. 'I hope they're not going to the pub with that huge machine,' Sally said. 'I haven't seen them around for a bit. I thought they'd left, or lost their licences.'

A little further on, after she'd heard the motor-bike start up she cried out, 'Dennis, my earring!' She put her hand to her left ear. 'Oh...my favourite earrings. I put them on tonight specially.' (He had given them to her at Christmas.) 'Oh I should have known better than to wear them to that crowded pub. I wonder if it came loose when I was doing my hair in the toilet? Look, I'll run back and at least tell Stan to ask the cleaner to look out for it.' He turned to come back with her. 'No, you better go on, because Susan might wonder where we are and she'll need to know we're not going to be late. I told her we'd be back about ten, and it's nearly that now. I'll be down there in a tick and I'll probably catch you up before you get to the top of the hill – you know how quickly I can walk – ' and she was round the corner and running on down as she said this, running frantically in order to be at the bar asking Stan or the bar maid about the earring as Tom pushed open the public bar door.

But she had to wait before she could catch the attention of anyone behind the bar because there was a crowd of people waiting to be served. She felt miserable and ashamed. Tom and his friends were not in the pub. She had lied and tricked for nothing. She hadn't meant to. It was entirely unpremeditated. She could leave now and catch Den up, show him the earring (handed to the barmaid from the lavatory) and her pleasure, and relief at his pleasure and relief, would be real. She would have salvaged the evening, got back to her proper place where she knew she was well and happy, escaped before everything crashed around her in a wreck. But having arranged all this, having got so far, she would wait and at least be seen to have a word with the barmaid or Stan. She would be glad to do that and then get out while she could, but it seemed an age they were taking. Then she was stuck and missed the moment when she could have turned and gone back out without being noticed.

Where the limited success in restricting the spread of malaria has been achieved it has been in rare cases where the will power in the patient and the desire to lead as normal a life as possible has been strong, strong enough for the discipline of protection to be kept up. The person infected can most successfully minimise the disorientating effects of the symptoms by accepting that the infection is chronic and taking measures, tried and trusty, according to the individual organism's experience, which minimise the affliction when it blossoms into acuteness, as it is bound to do from time to time. This is more effective than relying on the belief that they will not catch it again, and so becoming careless.

Finally she got through to the front of the bar and spoke to Stan. 'Last orders, please,' he was shouting, putting glasses and bottles on the bar with one hand, reaching behind him for cigarettes or crisps with the other, the three behind the bar moving to clear, serve and answer like the climax to a dance.

'No one's brought anything to me, but I'll tell the cleaner to look out for it.' She stretched her neck and turned her head for him to have a good look at the one still dangling from her right earlobe. As she did so she saw Tom go through the other bar and disappear into the back. 'Thank you, Stan. Sorry to be a nuisance. I'll just go and look again in the Ladies to make sure.' She now had to push back through the people crowding up to the bar behind her, hemming her in. There was a certain amount of banter which normally she would have joked her way out of, but she was flushed and rather near to tears as she said jerkily, 'Let me through, please. I'm in a hurry,' and dashed through the door that led to the toilets, put out by the laughter she heard, at her expense she was sure. And there was Tom at the phone in the passage. She was all dishevelled.

Why couldn't he have been there earlier when she was looking good? Had he seen her talking animatedly to Stan and come in here hoping she would? No, for he was talking on the phone, looked up when the door banged to see who had come in and then turned round away from her, hunched over the phone to hear clearer. His mouth was close to the mouthpiece and he was murmuring into it.

'Tom,' she got out. There had been no recognition as he had turned to the phone. Perhaps he hadn't known it was her, merely turned away from any recognition to feel private to make his phone call. He concentrated on the phone, refusing to look at her, talking urgently but not so she could hear any word, and fled back to his mates in the bar as soon as he put the receiver down.

She ran up the hill, crying and stumbling, and her chest hurt as she gasped for breath. By the time she got home she was quieter and trembling less, and cold shivering had set in. She crept exhausted into bed where she lay on the edge trying not to disturb Dennis with her attacks of shuddering. Then they lessened and she was leaden still, her silent tears soaking down into the pillow. Dennis, she thought, didn't wake.

Complications of malignant Tertian Malaria occur only in people with little or no acquired immunity to malaria; they are therefore seen particularly in visitors to malarious areas who have not taken a prophylactic anti-malarial drug and in people living in areas where there is good malaria control who nevertheless acquire the infection. Relapses of *P. vivax* and **P. orale** infection commonly recur for two years after the patient leaves a malarious area but are rare thereafter. *P. malariae* (quartan) infection may recur for five years or longer.

His mother agreed with Dennis that Sally must have caught cold coming out of the warm pub into the cold night air with only a light jacket on. She had seemed a bit feverish earlier that day Susan remembered. Spring was a tricky time. She'd probably been feeling the strain of Dennis working longer hours. Sally herself, coming downstairs on the third day to lie on the sofa and draw pictures with Jody, thought it might have been a meat pie she'd eaten for lunch, she had been so sick. Once she was over it she felt better than ever.

In the autumn of that year she and Susan were sorting out summer clothes making space in a cupboard for equipment for the baby due in two months' time. Before taking things to the cleaners they were going through pockets taking out bits of paper handkerchiefs and loose change and joking about finding five pound notes in Dennis' trousers. As Sally threw a handkerchief from a jacket pocket on to the pile for wash something dropped and chinked. Susan was by then in the kitchen and Sally ran down calling, 'Susan! Look! my earring!' and threw her arms round her mother-in-law's neck. 'The one I lost that night.' And later when Dennis came in she was wearing them both. 'Look, Den, I found it! Oh I am so glad to have it back.'

The new baby was a boy. Sally turned over deep within her possibilities of finding the name Thomas among relatives important to Susan and Dennis so that she would be able to say Tom's name whenever she wanted to but kept that thought to herself. At his brother Alan's birth it was thought a good idea for Jody to have a kitten. For Christmas Dennis had stuck a poster on the wall by Jody's bed of Tom Kitten, his favourite Beatrix Potter book, so he called his kitten Tomkitt.

Treatment

1. For acute attacks of Malaria the drug of choice is chloroquine.

2. For prevention of relapses the most effective drug for eradicating pre-erythrocytic forms of *P. vivax* and *P. malariae* is primaquine diphosphate.

3. Suppressive therapy is recommended for suppressing malaria during residence in an endemic area. Administration should start as soon as the area is entered and continue...

Cannibalism now and then

The disease of Kuru is fatal. It is a chronic degenerative disease of the central nervous system caused by a slow viral infection. It is carried only by humans among some of the peoples of Papua New Guinea.

The Fores are a tribe whose cannibalism is practised out of extreme devotion. They believe that if the spirit is not released from the corpse when a person dies, it will go to limbo. Greater love hath no man than this, that he lay down his life for his friend, and so to forestall this worst catastrophe that could befall anyone – being trapped in everlasting nothingness – they open the brain of the dead and eat it which is the only thing they know to do to release the spirit. Whether they also know that they will, as a result of their sacrificial act, die 'the laughing death' as it is called ('Kuru' in the Fore language means shivering or trembling which is one of the symptoms), willingly giving up their own lives and risking the fate of not being able to give up the ghost unless someone does the same easement for them, I have not been able to find out.

It should not be too difficult for quite different societies to understand this practice, both its impetus and its results, although it is to save their own souls rather than that of the person of whose flesh and blood they partake that the Christian makes sacramental communion.

Among people who consider themselves rational and of healthier habits than the Fores, the loving act has brought its revenges home many a time on the heads of those who intended nothing but good. No wonder that in more realistic ages than our own love was portrayed as a slayer. Cannibalism is still endemic in parts of the world. Who has not, in our own enlightened times, come across instances of rictus, of the clutch of some who love their families so dearly, wish their good and protection so nearly, that only by possession, by practically taking them back into their body do they feel they can keep them from harm; keep them close enough for them to receive only their own overwhelming love?

The effect of those absorbed in this way is usually for the spirit to be twisted up in chains, whereas with the Fore cannibal the mourning rituals are carried out expressly to let the spirit go and it is only for this that the people possess momentarily another's dead flesh, the living bodies taking over the toll of suffering so the dead may be free.

Butterfly

As the sun dried off the moisture from the outer leaves of the hedge the butterfly on the nettles moved its wings.

Babe. Silly name, but she wasn't silly. Oh, if that would work. It would make all the difference. It would change his life. It really would. One wave of the lucky wand. It could be so simple. Pictures of happiness supplanted the wretchedness of huddling in the wind, of always being disapproved of, bumping down the spiral of failure. To bring them to a nice clean flat. He would have toys for them there. They could spread out on the floor. They would shout and laugh and vie for his attention instead of being glum and whining to go home, and even if, as he knew from his experience of what the children always chose to do, they preferred to sit and watch television eating the sweets and sucking up the fizzy drink they used to make an expedition to the corner shop to get when he came in early enough to give them a coin or two from his pocket, it would at least be more comfortable and less expensive and less exhausting than pushing the baby in a wind that seemed to come at them from the cliff and the sea at one and the same time, with a miserable sniffly child clinging on to each of the cold steel sides of the push chair. If he could change that to an afternoon on a carpet with a bathroom handy and a kitchen where he could cook them tea, they would greet him clamorously when he came to fetch them, waving their arms to be picked up, wanting to show him things they had drawn, as they used to do. He would be favourite. He would watch Lisa's bliss as she scraped up the runny yellow of her egg with crisp fried bread. John II could make his paper models, which he was really very good at. They would ask to come again. They would seem to other people, passers-by, people in the café, to be happy likeable children and he, their competent father, would be included in the smiles of approval and attraction. They would have escaped from that slot, recognised from afar, of "problem". They would, instead, be wanted. They would be on the other side of the fence on the sunlit land.

The butterfly lay with its wings flat on the leaf so the colours and markings were visible and became strong in the light, and then it fluttered on its short inconsistent flights, flapping here and there where the flowers were opening to the warmth of the sun. A large patch of blue was expanding surprisingly quickly in the sky.

The insect lay on the flowers like a flower itself, palpitating its wings slightly as its proboscis dug for nectar.

He had yet to ask Marge. He'd have to choose his moment, that he knew now. She couldn't but be glad, though, if he had somewhere to take the children on their afternoon with him, if he didn't have to trail them up and down the promenade in the wind. Even in the weeks when the café was open for visitors, having an ice cream and a fizzy drink didn't fill up the whole afternoon. She had always complained that he wasn't prepared to do anything with the children only buy them off with sweets, filling them with what she called 'muck'. She'd said that if he hadn't any more imagination than that she'd stop the outings because Barney's catarrh was getting worse and she couldn't have him going down with bronchitis just because John must impose a father's wishes on them all. Why hadn't he had any 'father's wishes' when he lived there and they were only too available? Why hadn't he wanted to go out with them then?

He had certainly not wished to make the children ill or give her more work, and after that had expected not to be allowed to take them out next time. But they had been waiting as usual and Marge had not brought up that point further although poor Lisbeth's nose was running all the while, so it was he who said that as she seemed to have rather a bad cold shouldn't she stay at home, thinking to get his wife's approval by voicing an attitude of care he had learnt from her. But Marge had said fresh air didn't hurt a cold as long as they didn't stand about or unless he let them get soaked. There'd be no point in the others going if she had to keep the baby at home. Lisbeth would be more fretful without the others and it would just be more work for herself. And why should Lisbeth be left out of things just because she was the youngest and a girl?

The colour went out of the leaves as a cloud covered the sun.

What a stroke of luck then to have come across Babe. It had been by mere chance that he had mentioned his circumstances. Babe, who wanted to be helpful. She was out at work all day. As long as he left it straight, why shouldn't he use her flat an afternoon a week? she had said. Generous woman. That comparative strangers could be so kind and helpful while their own mother who should mind about their comfort...Babe had made things seem simple, as indeed they could be. If only he could just get into a patch where people thought easy the things that should be easy, like agreeing instead of jibing. A patch of luck, he supposed, would do it. Once one thing went your way, other luck seemed to come to it.

The cloud cleared the sun which stood in open sky. The heat increased. Then another cloud bank was pushed up and shadows swept like birds' wings over the hedges. The butterfly shut up its wings in the chill and became colourless.

Marge had the children all ready. He had always admired her efficiency about time. He wondered, though, how long they had been standing by the front door with scarves and gloves on so she should not lose a minute of the three hours without them; so there should be no possibility of him having to cross the threshold to wait while she found a woolly hat or accompanying teddy. It was impossible to mention anything about future arrangements. She was so plainly waiting, on one leg, so to speak, hand poised to shut the door after his departing back. Perhaps when he brought them back if the children looked clean and bright and didn't cry, and if she had had a good afternoon, she would ask him in for a cup of tea with all the pleasantness in the world when she felt like being kind, or even light-hearted, so that he forgot what she was like at other times, and wondered why in the world they couldn't go on living together. When she was sharp and unreasonable and scoring off him he could not remember that life had ever been anything other than miserable.

A buffet of wind reached the hedge. A leaf spilled its cache of water on to the plant below, drenching the butterfly.

'I can't have them going to another woman's flat. It was so you could spend time with them that I agreed to this arrangement, it's not particularly convenient for me, this once a week ritual. They take time to settle down again afterwards and of course it's me it comes back on. I thought you ought to see them but I don't want them just dumped in front of someone's telly and kept from worrying you with crisps and sweets while you spend your time drinking and smoking with your friends. I don't want them dragged into that sort of atmosphere.'

The butterfly struggled to open its wings. There was a patch near the body where the colour had been rubbed off. Some of the scales that formed the pattern had been damaged and the wings seemed to stick.

After work he went into the pub where he had spoken to Babe, where he had some acquaintance, but either the time in the evening was the unsociable time, or the particular night a quiet one for that pub. All the life of the place, the network of easy contact, the feeling of being at the juncture of possibly frequented roads, had disappeared. Two old women drinking bottled beer at a round table in a corner greeted a third who joined them but nobody else came in. He hadn't really wanted a drink, and certainly hadn't wished to afford out of his small funds the £2 for one for himself and the barman as an excuse for clinging on a bit longer in case someone who at least knew Babe, if not Babe herself, might come in. It might give the wrong impression, and so embarrass her, if he asked for news of her from the barman. He knew nothing of her circumstances after all. Almost certainly the man would not know where she lived, and John didn't even know her second name to enquire for her at her place of work, supposing that was known among the pub's clientèle. She might think it an intrusion, getting in touch with her at work. He would have to wait till he bumped into her by chance.

The butterfly crept on to the underside of a leaf. A cold shower came diagonally from a cloud like the emblems on an old map.

Among the envelopes put on the landing chest outside the room he rented there was not one from the local authority who had advertised for part-time evening help three nights a week in a residential home. He had filled in a lot of searching forms and got two referees for what would be a paltry job, but had thought he ought to try anything to earn a bit more money. He had not at all wanted to spend his evenings there but plainly they considered him not suitable even for that job. There was, however, a letter from an auctioneer's valuing the collection of pewter mugs he had taken to them, at £15. When he had thought of selling them he had thought of £150 – a friend had said he ought to get at least that – and had decided he would take as little as £100. £15! He felt as sore with disappointed expectancy as if it had been a calculated insult. Other people managed bits of business on the side. What was it he lacked, what trick, what luck?

He knew he was hungry but his one pan had yesterday's baked beans remains in, and he ate yet another cheese sandwich, used the gas ring to boil a kettle and went to bed with a stomach ache.

The rain ceased but the sky remained covered in cloud. More than most insects butterflies are dependent on sunshine for their survival. Few of them will fly and feed, much less mate and lay eggs, unless it is sunny.

When he felt less tired he must look for another room. He would be able to do much more in all sorts of ways if only he could make proper meals in a kitchen. He had gone home once with one of the other assistants in the shop. He had a tiny room at the top of a house, room only for a bed and cupboard and strewn with dirty clothes, but he had the use of a big light kitchen which had a table and chairs in, plants on the window-sill and a dresser full of crockery and pots and pans and a couple of easy chairs by a fireplace with a newish gas fire in it. There they had sat and had a good meal and talked and felt comfortable and sociable and it had seemed like being in a family house. For this week he would have to ring Marge and say he couldn't have the children on Thursday afternoon. He could say his half-day had been switched or that he was ill. No, not that he was ill. 'However bad I've felt I've managed to get the children to school. When could I ever go to bed when I had a stomach ache?'

The butterfly remained with its wings folded under the nettles. If a period of really bad weather happens to coincide with the flight period of a butterfly which is short-lived (and contrary to popular belief not all butterflies die after the legendary one day emergence to lay eggs; some even survive from one year to the next, and some cross oceans, travelling thousands of miles) this can have a disastrous effect on numbers and it may take years to build up the population again.

Ichneumon flies and butterflies

One of the best ways to stay alive is to become invisible. Some insects survive by becoming something else, which is what invisibility is, if you think about it, although the 'something else' is rarely 'air...thin air'. For example, the Viceroy Butterfly pretends to be a Monarch; the Milk Snake may in fact be a Grey-banded Kingsnake, and that in turn could really be a Coral Snake.

Fish have other sleights. Some can make themselves look bigger than they really are, or at least more dangerous. The Butterfly Fish makes a false eye to confuse followers – thus its name.

But against the Butterfly's most dangerous enemies – the ichneumon and parasitic flies – external appearance is no defence. The parasites, often tiny, lay their eggs either in the eggs or the larvae of butterflies and their grubs develop there, the host always perishing before it reaches maturity. The best-known of these butterfly parasites is the ichneumon fly Apanteles Glomeratus, and the Large White Butterfly is its prey.

Off the main street in local back street pubs that pride themselves on being 'family' pubs with a regular trade, friendly places that care about making people feel at home, you can recognise them, the barflies, on the *qui-vive* for likely prey. They do not hunt actively but, having selected a suitable environment, they station themselves for long stretches of the day in order to be in a favourable position should anything happen which they can make use of.

The etymology of ichneumon is in the dictionary traced through Ichnos: a track – ichneutic: of or relating to one who tracks or hunts, but your bar fly does not move much in a season unless another organism, inimical to him, appears in his chosen territory.

These are the sort of hostelleries which women on their own, now that they are getting on, now that they are on their own, have found a way of feeling comfortable enough in to frequent. Tea-shops or cheap restaurants open in the evening have largely disappeared, and cinemas where after a matinée one could go up the pile stairway walled with orange-tinted mirrors above shiny metal handrails to the restaurant and order a pot of tea and buttered scones sitting looking down on to the High Street from a small square table with a glass vase dead centre holding maximum five minimum four stems of flowers – these have entirely vanished. It is now many years since a person in winter could shorten the unpeopled sixteen hours of darkness by a poached egg on toast followed by a glass bowl of fruit salad (no cream, thank you, in the hope it might then be twopence less) and a little chat with the cashier at Joe Lyons or the ABC for a late and drawn out tea at six o'clock.

For if they have not a network of public activities left over from their earlier lives, if they do not have a church or a political party or a good cause to work for, or an older relative to visit and shop for, if they do not have lodgers or grandchildren to clean up after and prepare for, how else, apart from using the same shop and buying things they do not always need or want to afford, in order to get a nodding recognition from shopkeepers, are they to stitch the cloak of local acquaintanceship, net a fabric of existence in public, becoming visible to themselves because they are hailed by others?

Barfly is very economical in his expense of energy and effort, in what he notices or takes an interest in, but will seem a person of considerable resource, social awareness and concern to the new-comer for whom he exerts his one initial effort if he senses a possible source of succour.

He very often talks about his desire to better himself and be of use to others by changing his way of life. He admires the intelligence and culture and standards of his intended prey, recognising the chiming of refined sensibilities, appreciating originality and the attractiveness of a spirit free enough to recognise true worth. 'I can see you're no fool. You're not taken in by appearances.' At which unrealistic praise and sympathy, hesitantly, unaccustomedly, a tale of making do, of loneliness, of loss, of hard work, of saving, of savings, of plans, materialising at last after years of constriction, of perhaps going in with a friend to rent or buy a half-share in a caravan – a tale sweet to her ears because there was someone who found interesting what she had in her mind (who found it *very* interesting!) and because she had never put her life in words like this before.

So nice to come across someone not vulgarly mean, not carping and suspicious like so many who surround him in the life he has alas fallen upon, who, out of jealousy no doubt, wouldn't hesitate to warn her off becoming his friend, spread lies and slanders about him, because it's easy to hit a man when he's down, particularly when he's not one of the herd, is perhaps too independent of mind for them to quite accept him. 'I'll speak my mind, I will. I don't care who it is, if I think a thing's wrong, I'll say so. And I'll go so far as to say you're the type who'd do the same. They can bar me if they like. I'll give you an example...' (The people he has saved who cut him now, the good deeds he has done and got no credit for.) 'But I'm weak, I admit it. That's been my downfall. Too soft.' Once had other hopes, other possibilities and, frail creature, only human, down on his luck as he is, he still has faith in the human heart, still longing to change his ways and get back to a decent life. 'And I still feel that one day I will. You'd understand that, wouldn't you? I have the feeling you'd understand that. You've had some hard knocks, I should say – I'm sensitive that way – but you haven't let it get you down, have you? You've kept your head above water and got yourself together I'm sure.

'But you, my dear (cigarette? Here, let me) you've had the advantages of a better education. I can tell. I may look a scruff (actually, barfly is not at all badly dressed. He seems to have had the knack of being the same size as deceased husbands or brothers and as he is keen on his appearance people wanting someone to look after vie to be the special one to buy him presents; and then, since he spends all his money when he gets any, on himself he has some quite expensive gear) but I can tell style when I see it. And you, little lady, if you don't mind my saying so you have *style*.'

Although it has not been conclusively proved, it is very likely that parasites of this kind play an important role in the fluctuations of butterflies, and entomologists who have studied the subject carefully think that parasites may be largely to blame for the sudden dramatic disappearance of butterflies in localities where they have previously been numerous. As the butterfly population in some rather restricted locality increases so the conditions for parasites gradually improve and they too increase until they gain the ascendancy and become so numerous that very few of their host species escape destruction. This is tantamount to destroying their subsistence.

In some areas in recent years a hardier type of parasitic fly has emerged. Although it is still deeply engrained in some areas for a female to feel that in order to be regarded as successful she needs to be seen with, or known to have, a male (however awful), few young women now are prepared to pay the inflated price they formerly might have for the favour of being battened on and cadged from and sulked over, just as it became less likely that men, once they found they could get women to do the paying would continue to pod out to the exactions of floozies who made a living that way.

With the disappearance of their hosts, the parasites themselves decline and may even disappear from the locality (although Barnes and Wichett's claim in their latest paper that 'the time may soon be approaching when the non-occurrence of the conditions that favoured the Ichneumon will lead to their virtual disappearance' takes no account of the apparently exhaustless powers of adaptation and tenacity of the ichneumon). This new situation in any one small area gives the few remaining butterflies a chance to build up their numbers again which they may do if other conditions contribute. So a gradual re-population begins and continues until the same drama is played out once again after a period of years.

Out of synch

In order that the engine can run correctly, it is necessary for an electrical spark to ignite the fuel-air mixture in the combustion chamber at exactly the right moment in relation to engine speed and load.

She gave in, in her thoughts, and used the word 'love' in her comments to herself, that story we tell ourselves as we walk about reproducing our days, and us in them, for ourselves.

Whole seas over, singing inside, the sweetness of going with the warm current, the whole bay one glittering mass to float in, being borne along, sun beating down from the wide still sky. In, up to the neck in the high tide of love.

How easy everything was (why, because I'm in love of course, she told herself. That is what it means, in tune, at one, in synch with the world, meshed with what makes the world go round). All the problems that not being in love had presented her with, dissolved. She would twist and turn and look over her shoulder no further. This was her life then, the main stream of her life and she in it. Now longing to be back with him, she delayed in her walk past the frosty hedge-rows because she felt so sure of herself. She let herself get cold in the brown-pink frost of a winter's horizon at tea-time dusk because she would soon be warmed; and rather overwearied by having to go round further than she'd meant to, because he would revive her. The caravan's windows would send a stream of light to make a path across the rough grass of the field for her, she would run up the steps into his arms and tell him about the marvellous walk she'd had and the moment of truth, looking at the dun, dull, dead grasses and seeing them suddenly beautiful, irridescent, in a new light literally. She would tell him not to worry about last night that it didn't matter, really, it wasn't the most important thing. She would tell him how she had looked at the water in the ditch and the old man's beard curling like smoke over the hedges.

The ignition system is divided into two circuits, low tension and high tension. The LT or primary circuit consists of the battery, ignition switch, primary coil windings and the contact breaker points and condenser (at the distributor). The HT or secondary circuit consists of the secondary coil windings, the heavy ignition lead from the centre of the coil to the distributor cap, the rotor arm and the spark plug leads.

She could admit to him now that she had set out somewhat bleakly, feeling rather low and found the harsh winter afternoon and dun light and dead grasses at the edge of the wet fields suited her sadness. 'And then,' she heard her voice, with a little laugh in it, 'And then' (as if she were telling a child a story), and they would compare notes and she would say, 'And what were you thinking, Derek Beale, what were you feeling, let me see, at *exactly* ten to five?' for she had felt such a tingle, such a reverberation shoot through her that she had looked at her watch, which had a luminous dial, she felt hours might have passed. 'You know, Katie,' he would say, pushing the hair out of her eyes and rubbing her hands carefully between his to warm them, 'you really are extraordinary.'

The system is based on feeding low tension voltage from the battery to the coil where it is converted to high tension voltage. The high tension voltage is powerful enough to jump the spark plug gap in the cylinders many times a second under high compression pressures.

He would be waiting perhaps a little anxiously by now. Ah, but almost any adversity could be surmounted with the apprehension of love and a calm life ahead and he would find her cheerful and strong and they would support each other in being dependable, steadfast, good. And he would have tea ready to warm her, to thaw her loneliness, her distance and she would laugh and hold his poor face that had got chapped by the cold, and they would enjoy the feeling of closeness that being apart can bring to two people thinking the same thing, beating with the same rhythm, tuned.

The voltage will jump the gap and "spark" if the system is in good condition and all adjustments are correct.

She had left him to sleep off lunch in the caravan. They had not slept much the night before, their first night together for some months, not because it had been wonderful but because it had been unsatisfactory, and she had been disappointed when he didn't want to come a walk with her. But now she was glad, because she could tell him of her love.

The spark plug gap is of considerable importance as, if it is too large or too small the size of the spark and its efficiency will be seriously impaired and the engine will not "fire".

It must have been that damned liver for lunch. He supposed he never did feel really well away from home come to think of it. His bilious attack must have been coming on last night. That could account for his lack of performance. Oh lord, well, they'd have to stay till Thursday now. It wouldn't do to make the family think anything other than that his bi-monthly inspection had caused him to be away the usual two days. If he turned up tomorrow he would have to fabricate an explanation, talk about it, lie verbally rather than by implication, which made all the difference. And it would make it all seem too important to Kate if he suddenly changed their arrangements, too emotional. If he said they had to go because it wasn't as they'd anticipated she'd want to discuss the situation, want to know why and what next and when and how, and say she still wanted him for a friend whether there was bed or not – oh no, he wasn't going to land himself in any of that. It hadn't worked. The sooner he could forget about his lapse the better. He really was more comfortable at home. He'd suggest a concert to Fiona when he got home – or just get the tickets. That would please her. A surprise. More romantic. Women like surprises.

If Kate had come that first time he'd suggested it, when he was really excited about having this affair, perhaps he could have given her a better time. He would have liked to have someone to spend his loving on, to write intimate letters to, talk to, tell his feelings to, be gallant to, an outlet for a bit of style. Small chance of any of that in his household of four boys. Fiona was the one who took charge at home, of course. He needed that for the base of his life – but he would have liked to supply this bright young girl with some adulation and kindness, some attention, make her feel cared for which it seemed she had lacked prior to taking up with him; whereas his busy wife rather mocked his efforts at gracious living. 'You *are* the Gay Lothario today,' she'd sometimes say almost brushing him up with the crumbs if he wanted to sit on after breakfast and talk about the state of his feelings when he didn't have to get to the Institute till the afternoon. She had the boys' adventures to listen to now. She always showed an interest in their rather tedious anxieties and discussions of the intellectual fashions among their school and college friends.

In the story we tell ourselves, and from which we occasionally select rehearsed quotations to tell others, to make us real to ourselves, he would have liked to be able still to use certain phrases: 'an affair with a younger woman, a full-blooded – a *very* full-blooded – carnal affair. New lease of life. She's absobloodylutely marvellous,' but the fibres in his body if not acknowledged by his conscious mind recognised that words and thoughts of his family, scenes from his life, were pushing in when they were just not in existence on the scene when he'd first decided to proposition Kate. It was her fault for not accepting him when the opportunity was right; for giving him time to have difficulties about it.

When refitting the spark plugs, make sure that they are tightened to the specified torque and that the leads are refitted in the correct firing order.

She came up the steps of the caravan singing. When she opened the door on to darkness she realised she had been disappointed that he had not been looking out to welcome her, or put the light on to light her across the field, wondering where she'd got to, impatient as she was for her to be there. She had had words ready to soothe his anxiety that she might have got lost and cold; she was going to give him reassurance that she was not fussy, not going to be a nuisance to him. She had felt so near him, so close in thought when she was alone across the fields, so sure of the telepathy between them, their feelings and thoughts chiming as one.

Fault diagnosis – ignition system
  By far the majority of breakdowns and running troubles are caused by faults in the ignition system, either in the low tension or high tension circuits.

He had his back to her all humped round on the far side of the double bunk. She went to caress him and snuggle up and whisper her secrets, though it would have been nice if he'd had tea ready. She'd come in with him now if that's what he wanted, though they'd had all last night when he didn't. When she touched his shoulder he twitched it irritably and curled more into himself with a sleepy groan. 'What's the matter?' He was relieved to recognise the concern of good feeling not of reprimand in her voice. She was not going to be cross and need an effort to mollify then, so he would not restrain his ill-temper. It would help block off any prising enquiries. 'Nothing. I'm just tired, that's all. I don't think the lunch agreed with me. I'm not sure that liver wasn't a bit off.'
  'I'll make some tea shall I?' 'If you like.' 'It was quite cold out. I got a little bit lost. I could do with some tea myself. To warm up. I think it's going to be a cold night. Are you cold?' 'Hadn't thought about it.' He concentrated on keeping still, pretending to be drowsy.

  Loss of power and overheating, apart from faulty carburation settings, are normally due to faults in the distributor or to incorrect ignition timing.

She went down the steps again to empty the teapot and round the corner of the caravan she cried, biting back the sobs so that he should not hear and be upset. 'Perhaps if I stay here a bit he will come and see if I'm all right,' she thought, but knew she could stay out there all night for all he'd really miss her, only annoyed, perhaps, that he had to come and look for her.
  She shook the teapot out, gave a big sniff – she wasn't going to be a burden, one of those fussy hysterical females, after all she'd known he wasn't in a position for her to depend on him as he would have liked, no clinging vine, she. Perhaps if he had a good sleep he'd feel better and they'd go a walk tomorrow and be communicative and delight each other again with their company. She went up the steps of the caravan with tired legs. On the top step she looked over the wintry fields, and the hedges whose beauty in the frost she had felt to be so suited to her own peace

and joy, to the harmony of their feelings chiming together. Moonlight was beginning to blacken them and steepen the shadows of the track where she had walked between the frozen ditches. An owl hooted and some small non-predatory animal screamed its death-cry from the copse that backed the field the caravan was in. The land and the night over the land was becoming alien and frightening. Something had gone wrong so the time they had made to be together – two whole nights, mornings, afternoons, evenings was not what it should have been. She didn't understand what had annoyed him so in her behaviour when the love which he had set flowing was so plentifully there for him.

If the ignition timing is too far retarded, it should be noted that the engine will tend to overheat and there will be quite a noticeable drop in power. (If however this loss occurs and, on checking, the ignition timing is found to be correct, you should check the carburettor, where the fault may lie.) (For details of the fuel and exhaust systems see chapter 3 – fault diagnosis: section 19.)

Empty trucks

As children we used to run up the slope to the railway bridge, however unwilling we'd been to go the walk, tired, lagging, no doubt infuriatingly so to adults who had things planned for after tea and were fed up with waiting at every stile for the slowcoach.

We wanted not to miss the goods trains. Sometimes we got one, forty-eight trucks all full, large lumps of coal gleaming in the rain, big as rocks, sometimes what May, who took us on these walks, told us was 'antracite' – dusty piles of grit. Sometimes it was grit and sand in the trucks for the builder's yard by the station.

The real bull's eye was if we got there when the empty trucks were going back down the line again after delivery. For one thing they made a quite different noise. You could hear the echo of them being banged into each other as they were shunted for the engine to come and collect them. Joe, who was a know-all and liked to show off his ideas for improving the world (usually something he'd heard Dad say when our parents were discussing the news at breakfast), said that they shouldn't go back empty. It wasn't gnomic. They could be filled with something else that needed to go the other way.

I saw endless complications in this. For instance, if it wasn't coal you were taking back (which would be silly as it had just come) you would have to scrub out the trucks which were engrimed with a lifetime's coal dust. To get one little bird box clean enough to put chickens in was difficult enough and I felt quite weary at the thought of scrubbing out the trucks. It would be like one of those tasks set by witches in stories, like emptying a huge lake with a thimble by the time she came back in an hour at sunset, impossible without some magic saving agency. But I didn't discuss alternatives with my brother who had a right to know more than me because he was older, as he always had an answer that dismissed what I said. 'Until you have the facts at your fingertips you shouldn't speculate' was at that time his clinching phrase, picked up I suppose from some teacher at his school. When I tried it on him it didn't work. Naturally it was mainly on me who believed him that he tried out these phrases.

But I liked the empty trucks, and so, of course, did he. They swayed and clunked and rattled and if we had got to the bridge in time you sometimes saw strange things in them, bits of wood, a wheel, bits of machinery, tarpaulins with letters stamped on them and beautifully plaited bits of cord round brass eyelets in the corners. Once there was an old pram, with a torn hood all lopsided and it bobbed up and down with the movement of the truck. We couldn't see if there was a baby in it. May said not. Even better, once there was a man asleep on a tarpaulin. He had an old coat over him and you could see his feet at the bottom and a shaggy head of hair and beard and his arms at the top and his trousers spread out drying in the sun beside him and his boots. He had a blue enamel can with a handle and a lid and some brown bottles that were rolling on their side in a dip in the tarpaulin. Joe said his trousers probably would be dry by the time the train got back to Wales, which is where he reckoned it was going. To go across the whole of England right to Wales in such sunny privacy, to see the whole of England going by from such privileged secrecy, this became my ideal as a way of travelling, as a way of life, for some time after, although Joe did manage to dim it a bit by saying that if no one could see you (except birds and pilots of aeroplanes, and people on bridges like us) then you wouldn't be able to see anything but the sky either.

A very old and ugly person came to the school I went to to talk at Speech Day. She was quite important apparently and someone said she was a pioneer, though she didn't talk about exploring or geography. I remember one thing she said. Like most people she was on about making the most of our opportunities, but the bit I remember was what she said about time, because it was more or less what May used to say when she wanted us to get a move on which I'd never taken much notice of as it was only May going on. She told us a rhyme or poem which I liked because it was rather sad. She said her grandmother when she was a little girl had sewn it in cross-stitch on a piece of cloth, and she as a child had looked at it every meal-time because it was on the wall opposite where she sat. Her voice quivered a bit at the last line.

Lost, yesterday, somewhere between sunrise and sunset
Two golden hours, each set with sixty diamond minutes.
No reward is offered, for they are gone forever.

So when I think about wasting time or 'living in the present' which we are often advised to do by all sorts of people, or when I am kindly told by my brother Joseph on his occasional visits (my brother Joseph has done very well in engineering, so well that he has had to learn how to relax and take holidays since a heart attack) not to overload myself looking after two families and trying to run the remains of our parents' business, then the walks, and May's voice saying we'd got to watch the time, come into my mind, and the rhyme that that prestigious old dragon who'd apparently battled to have the Women's Property Act or something brought in, told us.

And I see each 'now' we are trying to keep and hoard and fill and load with value, disappearing empty and unused like the coal trucks going back down the line after delivery, being shunted and moving slowly down the track, echoing more and more distantly as the train disappears round the hill until all is quiet again, and the rail shines on in the heat as far as you could see to the horizon, and even the last trace of smoke had gone from the empty blue sky.

House in a wood

'…there are some moods like houses, long unvisited…'

We went up the steps to the house. It was long unvisited. We walked up lightly as if we came there frequently, in daily life, like going into the baker's.

But it had been years, another life, since we had even been in the neighbourhood, into the woods; or indeed taken any Sunday afternoon walk, exploring, looking about us, noticing for the next time; it had been another life in which then returning home across the frosting fields with a smoking pink horizon fading like a wisp of fire behind us, we came in to tea at dusk, curtain drawn bright fire. Passed as a dream, that time; and like a dream sometimes suddenly that time jumped fully clothed in all its detail unaccountably in the path of our day.

Groundsel and tufts of grass were growing in the corners of the steps. Lichen and moss on one of the balustrades had flaked patches of the stone. There was no tumbled rubble to push our feet through though. The steps were in surprisingly good condition. The door opened with a light push and we held our breaths for what waft of fungus coming up from skeleton joists, what dead rats, bundles of rotting rags, blackened cans, broken bottles at the edge of circles of ash and half-burnt parts of chairs; what results of neglect and absence.

But we walked into a furnished house. It was uninhabited but not empty, the rooms, like moods, biding their time, available.

We could have come here at any time just like this so easily. Why, we wondered then, had we not done so simple and desirable a thing? It must have been that it seemed we could not.

Friends, keep your establishment. For much of the time I have not been very far though often thrown wide by the network of paths and earthworks; misguided by seeming tracks, distracted from your centre, distrained, it must have seemed to me then. One winter afternoon as dark comes down and you settle to the fire and the room and shut out the night and the night's inhabitants, forbear to draw the curtains on the side window that looks across the garden to the wood. The light and the movement of the fire will show me where I am, and easily, naturally – long-unvisited friends – I will walk up the steps and find myself with you.

Photograph

You can change the details on a photograph. You can do trick photography to put a mini-skirt on a 1930s sepia bathing belle. In this version different weather blows out over the line of the coast that in that print was a picture in the sun before they built the power station. A figure emerges through the trees, a ghost called up by a smudge on the negative, tampering with time by making a mark on space.

And here on the floor is sat a small solid triangle. No flowery baby's dress, no woolly rug or black velvet background, brushed hair and ribbon, no Chippendale on which stands perfectly central and polished, the polish reflected in the polished table, the rose bowl for calling cards.

The photographer carried his heavy gear back out of the trades-men's entrance long ago, but the floppy raised paw, the sideways glance up, the 'when-will-they-find-out?' look that he captured half a century ago has come out on this recent snap in the huge batch of prints we've just collected from Boots. A delayed mecha-nism indeed, an image re-turned, a double exposure.

It is as if one of the old batch had got mislaid and arrived now, the disappearance of the village shop fronts – the haberdashers, the hairdressers with a pale green model of 'Eugene' in the window in what was then a side-road, the ironmongers, the photographer's studio, next to the coal office on the slope up from the station – notwithstanding. As if 'Clearing out, we came across this old neg-ative. We thought you might like to have it.' As if two negatives got superimposed, some details of pattern in the cloth so strong that it came through the dye. Delayed process indeed, double exposure with the past showing through the present like a shadow on the lense.

The snap is of a new baby crowded round with adoring people for her first birthday. It is not a 'once upon a time' background but our untidy living room, our little lump of love sitting there, sly half-smile and great blue gaze ('What *is* it you've got there? Come on, give to Mummy') reaching me across fifty years.

Soon she'll get Russian dolls for Christmas; and move up one size in twenty years' time.

Beeches

Layered like water, the beeches, a great bank in the sky.

What a peaceful inbetween morning, taking time to clear up, coasting, retrieving, on each round of house and yard more things seen to each time strands separated from the general tangle, things going back into place after full house, after everything brought out, used, used up. And time enough to leave it and yet do it all before Sheila came in at four.

The separate leaves are one spray, the direction of branches one shape to the eye.

And it was only the night before last they suddenly found themselves on grey plastic chairs at the top of a building, long carpeted corridors, at a jazz club of all things, among devotees; totally unexpected. Jack had had tickets to spare and bumping into him on the way to the dentist had been a surprise. They had dressed up a bit – velvets – been part of the swing. Their neighbours here only knew them in old clothes. A different world, they would have said.

The limbs of the tree move within a curve traced on the sky. The green circle a child makes in a picture is not so far off.

Yesterday – was it only yesterday? waking up early in Town it seemed another age – they had each gone to do bits of business. Sheila had been to see her mother and dealt with the tickets on the way. What they'd covered between them by the time they met at Kennington! – food collected, passports seen to, and they got to the Hoskissons', the borrowed cat basket and all, jump on time; even fitted in a free sherry and a greeting at Benny's preview. Sheila, to the Hoskissons, referred to it as a 'vernissage'. She had peered absorbedly at the three or four plaques set at angles on the walls – although it was only a few friends and B's mother and sister in a back basement room. Sheila did rather love to do different acts. She was not really a snob, she just had this facility for joining in whoever she was with, a sort of aligning herself out of courtesy, as well as wanting to be king pin.

There is one separate beech a little to the side with branches delicately held out.

Then out of Town they had gone, the four of them and the cat, the jallopy packed with their friends, bags of supplies, tools, papers, Hoskissons' cat delivered on the way, out of Town before the light quite faded in the sky behind them.

It may look separate according to where you are standing.

Leaving the cat at the vet's had slightly disturbed their feeling of all going well, of competence, of managing everything like practised jugglers. Not the cat's behaviour – the Hoskie's Marigold had nerves of steel – but the young woman in a white coat who opened the door. Something scornful and personal about her as if she was a doctor in trouble. Strange atmosphere. That particular little splinter of yesterday's world had almost been swallowed up in the dark, so separate was it, so out of key with the pleasure of the journey, the beauty of the evening landscape, their arrival back home, the smell of the garden, the letters, settling in, making up beds, the Hoskisson's pleasure at the place. They had gone in the dark to take the cat up a gravel drive with rhododendrons. It was like a dream or film to think of now in morning light leaning against the sink looking across to the beeches.

The lower branch of leaves is held out, is still, a lacy canopy of leaves, almost mirrored by the next spread above it. Usually you think of a tree's branch mirrored in water below, not by air above.

The Hoskissons were looking forward to their crossing. Above all being able to provide them with something of use to them – not a thought-up occasion stiffly to keep in touch, rightly to repay hospitality and kindness, but being with them in the course of their own life. Easy to suggest that they break their journey to the coast, take pot luck with them, not a special invitation with expectations. They had rested. It had been a good evening. Sheila had taken them off first thing to the station. Now the house and the day were disentangling themselves from the hubbub of the last two days. They themselves would not be going on their holiday for another month – that again was a whole other – ball-game was it the Americans said? If they said that when they got there would they stand out as old-fashioned? The Hoskissons didn't know they were going to America. Another life, but twined, but twinned. Strange eyes that woman had had. The kitchen floor was done. Now for the hedge. The clippers were in their place in the shed – and oh there was a long lingering sort-out of that shed ahead of them. They could settle down to that tomorrow evening. The frames had been promised to old Benson, must remember that. Tomorrow. There was not a mark on the laid-out sheet of tomorrow yet. It was all coming together. Sheila would be in soon.

The spread of the branches is as if layered in water but held apart by the layers of air; yet to the eye from over the field they all sway in unison to the wind. The trunks remain still but the great beech hedge in the sky sways, moves, swirls, one banked mass against the thin space of the sky.

Like a wave breaking

He let himself into the house in the early hours of a summer morning coming off nightshift when the sky was an overall light grey before dawn struck it with its rays from the horizon. The household was sleeping, the doors on to the landing open and the sound of the children's regular breathing quite audible. The tattered old velvet curtains had been drawn across the French windows and the sitting room was a pool of warm darkness within them.

As he paused on the threshold to the room before tiptoeing upstairs he felt the day standing waiting behind the fold of the curtain, like a person listening at a door, attending to the stirrings in the house as he was, adding the slight shiver of a dawn wind freshening up the night.

It was waiting suspended but on its way, like a wave – like a wave curling over just before it descends
like a wave about to break, throwing itself down all along the shore in a splashing moving dancing line of points of shining white.

If he was to get any sleep he must slip upstairs before that wave crashed, before the gong of the sun boomed from above the horizon, showering every surface, every nook and cranny, inexorably with the light of day breaking.

Ahead, behind

The kite leapt up clear of the ground over a puff of wind. It moved up, straightening the string. 'Let me, let me,' the child beside the man begged to hold it. The adult paid out more string and when the kite was high and stable above them, riding the air, leaning hard on it, gave the bar to the child to hold. The child was drawn with a jerk over the grass, the kite stronger than he had thought. He ran faster than he knew how, screaming and laughing, getting used to paying out more string, when to pull down with the hand, when not to resist. Up to the crown of the rolling hill he rushed, half-resistant tugged half running forward into the pull of the kite, urging it on.

By the time they had to go the wind was dropping. The kite was lower and needed the longer arm of the man to manipulate and keep it from flopping. The child was tired. You could see now what a large heavy kite it was, with different sections and many streamers attached, cumbersome like a bird that is heavy and clumsy on land, swift and vivid aloft. The man pulled the complicated structure after him as they started to make their way slowly and steadily home.

The tunnel and the open

While you are out in the sunlight it is all right, it is quite right, that you sway about, straggle, dart from one side to the other, now pausing with someone to look over the valley now rushing across to catch up with friends, linking arms, fooling about, irregularly here and there, mucking about, huffing and puffing if the going's hard, stopping for a rest, wondering which way, whether to go on or divagate; going in the general direction forward along with everyone else, but in fits and starts, not concentrating, plenty of leeway, plenty of time, visibility good on solid ground where you can see the roads and which ways they go.

But, once you are in the tunnel keep your hands steady, steady on the wheel; or at even distance touching your finger on the wall for balance, your feet straight and going straight ahead with regular step, one before the other, right foot, left foot one in the space just ahead of the other, leaving no gap in which to trip, leaving no space of time in which to balk direction – evenly, keeping the footway.

The air gets sparse in the tunnel, you cannot afford one wasteful draining unnecessary movement. If you stop if you feel dizzy, you may lose your direction. You cannot depend on your senses, only on the habit of your muscles. You put one foot before the other, you keep your hands steady on the wheel or at the same distance from the wall going at an even pace in order that your heart shall continue to beat regularly, the blood with oxygen continue to circulate without interruption you keep going to keep going.

The tunnel may have an opening the other end. The beat, beat and plod of one foot in front of the other clip clop evenly on the unguessable floor (sand? chalk, slippery, pebbly, will there be puddles?) will suddenly in an uninterrupted swing forward place one foot, the front of your body, on grass in sunlight; you have come out into a meadow into daylight or a busy road in broad midday, everyone thronging to Town. But just as likely, more likely from the way you taste this dark on your tongue up against the back of your teeth, it goes on as it is slightly declining, deepening darkening down and darker, but all you can do is push on as before one foot in front of the other, evenly, hands steady on the wheel while there is a wheel to hold, a road to walk while the walking makes the road, the holding the wheel to keep the wheels steady in the track makes the space whereby we can push through, go on.

Time yet

Dark lighter, dun dark relieved sunny obscured, and settled dark again.

A level patch of ground on the hillside across the valley had trapped the snow and shone with a brown-yellowish light through the dusk of a winter afternoon. Fitful gleams were passing high up behind the moving clouds, the air thickening with snow, rearranging, filling up the sky, until the play – the balance of light shining across, and being snuffed out – was suddenly finished and the air came down uniform a little above our heads as thick falling snow.

So we dally, thinking the to and fro, the darting out sinking low and gradual strengthening again of energy and activity will go on consistently, that there will be time yet, daylight yet, our morning chances still there. And suddenly the light has gone and we find we had better hurry home.

A candle flame deprived of air

The blue swelling on the tip of the wick quickly climbed into a wavering yellow flame, elongating and pulsating. After a rapid shrinking it rose back a little and settled to a steady cone of light, the yellow surround and the smoky arch within it now of constant proportion. The wall was bathed in a soft clear yellow without shadow.

You put a glass over it to show the child that the candle needs air.

The flame remains but instantly loses its light. It darkens, it sickens, diminishes. It shrinks into itself. It is gone.

The man said very little latterly on his errands to get bread, to pay bills. Then he ceased to go out, though occasionally seen, standing in his open back door, once or twice getting in washing. Then no doors or windows were opened, the curtains hardly ever drawn back. When he first restricted his habitation to his room at the top of the house he yet sat at the table, lit the gas fire, made tea, got up and went to bed. The period was short when he remained in his bed and yet used it like a boat's cabin: reading lamp, tray for food, different positions, sitting up in the day, lying down for sleep. Soon he had pushed it all away and lay, the progress of the day not reaching his shadowed recess, tossing and turning sometimes though moving as if in an attempt to shift a burden from his chest, to get air. Once turned on his side facing the wall he did not turn back. He lay quite still. Gradually his knees started to move up and his shoulders shrank down as if a caterpillar should very slowly turn in on itself. When his right elbow was on his knee and his head pushed into the crook of his arm beneath the stale blankets in the airless dark there was no further movement he could make.

The spindle unwinds, winds, unwinds

As over the high passes where snow is dense, the soft air tunnels a route, blunting with warmth the sharp edges of ice-blocks that have been frozen solid all winter

so spring opens roads into the night, riddling the thick impenetrable dark with lifting grey as if it were a gauze network whose channels once advanced feel their way to open spaces, vistas (though within the border of the wood you are unseen from the field) making the tract viable;

and so the same, when the year has again crossed over, dipping to the diagonal, the beams will become shorter, pulling in, broader and blunter, breaking off against the wall of the forest, the days – wavelets of a receding tide getting shorter and shorter, their reach up the sand feebler and feebler until

long night, the long untouched closed territory of night is here again.

Relative matter of extension

As a pile of fleece can be pulled out and spun into a long continuous thread

and a tank of liquid petroleum be stretched out and twisted until the globules have become a nylon thread as fine as a spider's filament;

as the flayed skin laid flat – once the covering of a standing animal, three-dimensional – can become an unbroken thong by cutting round and round the diameter with a sharp knife

and a lump of clay can be kneaded and rolled out into a long snake;

so too can the yarn be knitted into a piece and made into a coat again

and the thread too fine to be visible in air netted into a fabric to barricade an estuary and become a shining surface again.

So mass becomes length which is space condensed to mass again

and the thong which Hengist and Horsa tricked out of the bullock's hide surrounds a city.

What is a path but space condensed and spun out, space arrowed to its target, distance? Space is drawn out into a line as a thread from a mass, and once linear turns into direction

which if we follow we can hold within us and throw a net round distance.

Solstices

Swing up round into the dark nook by the wall, out of hot baked glare on the road into dark under the copper beech on the corner, then on into light again, the car going on up until the next swing round into the open, the heat-hazed valley all laid open below, and round and up again, gears changing beautifully, round and along and up again into the high hot clear air, making for home, known pleasures, lovely, lovely day

nothing more to do, absolute. Heat, midday, full, summer.

And could death be like this – apogee – a finishing, a perfection, a finale and held note on the major of cold iced sun, for death is cold but in no other way may need to be different; burst of a completed sun, burst and unwavering beam of the dark dazzle off the freeze, as this off the white light of summer? Absolute, nothing more to do, laid open.

Why not?

Happy in the summer, joyful greeting in shaded streets of even strangers on their way to things; the explosion of the poppy as it shoots its bolt, balanced pole, quivering needle stayed at the upright before it slides down again

On the same axis lies the other Pole, the ending, the release, the last tender touching of the fading face, communion of even strangers over the finishing, the clutch relaxed, nothing left to do, laid down; for the line that goes through it is the one line through all three points, fulcrum and Poles. Swing down, ease down, away from the needles exploding from the cold, into the shade, then further down through cold again, down, away – the same point of attainment, of halt, of rest reached after all the oscillation in between.

A gift of flowers

The gift of flowers, the bowl of the tulip like the comfort of a sympathetic child's hand on the taut face, on the wracked head, cup-like little hand, healing;

the gift of flowers, the spray of mignonette like the eyes that fill with tears at your sorrow;

the gift of flowers, a person who crosses the room and says come with me I'm going your way I'll get you home.

And I look now at the stubby point of the iris, the white blobs which are carnation buds, a few tinged with pink opening out, flecked with pink on the back side of the opening frilled petal, and the spray of three buds leaning on the other side against the wall, and the fuzzy blue, in the dusk of that part of the room on the mantelpiece only blue because I know it's blue,

a loving-one's flowers, as if to say, 'Don't give up, don't stop doing kind things, don't give in to the warping world, there are other sorts. The harm these tyrannies do is to make you see the world like that. There are other things. People can spit poison at you, but people can give you comfort. There are healings, there are joys. Here are some flowers.'

Cup of milk

A trickle which if spilt would only make a puddle on the table, opaque wetness held between the ribs of the worn wood on this old table – lees which if rinsed out in the sink would make only thinly milky, grey-white, a pint of water, if you yet pour it into this small cup makes a globe of milk.

This chunky solid bulbous coffee-cup you can hold in the curled palm of your hand as an egg in an eggcup. The drop of milk fills this small cup just rightly to the brim as the cup fills your hand, nourishment not waste, full white infill, cup used for holding, not space prone to shadow and bits falling in but cup of fullness, cup of achievement, same quantity vehicle and content.

Hold the cup steady in your hand, each hour as it falls softly through the day easy with activities: chopping wood on a fine day, cleaning a bit, the letter written, information garnered, the errands to pay bills, deliver things; food prepared, stores laid in, the drop saved against another round tomorrow, actions laid up against the dark. Hold the cup steady,

and at the right time if the swing of the axe is right in conjunction with its angle the wood splits into soldiers almost of itself. You do not need to flail if you let it drop right – poise and let drop, as the hours fall with a quiet but firm settling (moving in rhythm as drifting leaves find definitely their proper place if the swaying is not disturbed by intrusion of thwart winds);

at that moment which is recognised rather than known, rather than decided on, rather than aimed at, without thought, but in an interval of concentration between thought;

as if in libation, but not jettisoned,

lift it to your lips and drink.

Shawls

We walked into the garden as day lifted the sky and here and there on the dark hedges lay white patches, fine wool stuff soaking wet with droplets that made them seem shrunken pieces of fallen mist, like little bits of out-of-place snow still solid when the field round it is warm and green again, finest fairy wool stuff pieces spread to whiten under the dry moon and caught by the danks and darks of night.

Only close up did you see the thousand threads of the fabric, large cobwebs visibly engorged by the wet on them.

It was as if shawls of lightest wool, the softest merino, had been placed here and there delicately with no pressure, no weight on tired bones, as when the gentleness of love puts with a light touch a fine scarf round frail shoulders baby-soft fabric nestling up to gossamer wisps of white hair.

Some gentle love had floated down these drifts, these shawls of dew and they remained there undisturbed on the dark evergreens well into the clear day.

...first.
—en or the egg, chick–?

'She's doing fine. There's absolutely nothing to worry about. Perfectly normal. It won't be long now but why don't you go and have a cup of tea in the canteen while you've got the chance? Get a nice hot cup and drink it slowly. I should say you've got at least another 20 minutes.

Come on now, keep at it, you mustn't go to sleep now. Push. Easy now, whoah there, gently now, one more push, nearly there.'

'...and if you make Market Street one way going north you can route the traffic for Macclesfield out of the town at this junction, southbound traffic being deflected to the east of Cuthbert Square, thus releasing...'

'...should give her a ground floor...'

'...can assure the Honourable Member that the Foreign Secretary is doing his utmost to make our position clear on this matter, and when I say "our" I mean not only that of this government but that of the people of Great Britain as a whole, that while we will do everything in our power to help bring about peaceful negotiations, we must never, never...'

'...Those in favour?...Thank you. Those against?...Thank you. Passed unanimously. Now, as to the question of charitable status raised under A.O.B. our Treasurer, Mrs Bone, has, I believe, some information to give us. Mrs Bone...'

'I should strip the wallpaper off first before you buy the paint because the condition of the wall...goodness knows what you might find underneath all those layers. They've just slapped a new more hideous one of top of the old. Look at this. If you could get that off in one piece I should think the V. and A. would have it. On the other hand it might be...'

'...And I say we cannot continue to employ someone who upsets the managers, however efficient...'

'Has it come then? Is it all right?'
'Yes, a beautiful baby. Well done. A lovely little boy. You can rest now.'

'all this central part shaded beige on the map for...'

'flat at least now there's a baby if they can't transfer her to a house which they ought to do.'

'give in to this kind of pressure which is tantamount to blackmail of the most blatant kind. And whereas we agree, of course we agree, that the terms of the international agreement on underwater exploration must be adhered to...'

'Yes, well, since our last meeting I've looked into this and...'

'holding up the wall so you better go carefully.'

'he may be. You cannot overlook the feelings of the people who are actually on the spot running these shops. They know the area and the clientèle. You can't have an outsider coming in brushing aside their grass-roots experience. Mr Chadhuri himself told me – yes, Station Road, Croydon outlet, that's the one...'

'I'm sorry I couldn't get here earlier. How is he?'
'His breathing seems a little easier. He slept this morning for an hour. He's been in agony but he's more coherent than he's

been for days. He seems a bit easier now. They've stopped the morphine. He knows you're coming.'

The grey papery scaly face wrinkled into smiles and the glazed eyes shone. 'All the way from Canadie, Cherry, all the way across the sea,' he wheezed and mumbled. 'All the w– ti-tumt...coss the sse...'. The mouth slurred shut. With his bony twisted claw in the warm hand of the living, the old man went.

'Who's Cherry? Was he trying to say Charlie?'

'I think he used to call his mother Cherry, from a song or a sort of game. He was trying to sing to the nurse yesterday. Marvellous these nurses. She understood. She knew he was going even though he seemed better to us.'

'So he didn't recognise me after all.'

'Oh I think he did. The name doesn't matter. He connected all right. He knew you, who you were. Will you come home with me? I'm going there now.'

They came down from the fifth floor through the maze that the continuously expanding hospital had become. The last corridor before they got out to the car park was in an outer wing and by no means quiet. There was a continual hubbub, the noise of wheels of trolleys and cots and surgical trays and voices and people from outside in coats talking as if they were in the street. A nurse went up to a man fidgeting at the end of the corridor. 'You can come in now Mr Baines. Yes, everything's fine. You've got a lovely little...'

'...but really they ought to have...'

'...the body of a child...'

'...Whatever happens we must make it absolutely clear...'

'...Oh, what a pretty colour...'

'...and we should like to thank, on behalf of all our members...'

'...But you do see, Mrs Stokes, don't you, that we really can't have the whole school being disrupted by...'

GUATAMALA – time to act

'...was found early on Saturday morning by the side of the tow-path two miles upstream from Chertsey Lock by a man walking his dog.'

> Escaped prisoner found cooking kippers in
> Epping Forest three weeks after break-out.

'It's going to rain all day. Come on, get the cards out and we'll have some tea and go another day. You deal.'

Seven sentences

The young cat put the bird it had killed on the doorstep and then lay slumped for hours as apparently without life as a fur on a coat dropped on the floor.

They heard neither rain nor clock nor the crepitations of the thoughts that had wrought them a little while before, but lay together oblivious on the other side of sleep, no itch, no tossing, no nerve or limb restless, skin relaxed round bone, the knot untangled, the band loosed, the life dispensed.

As the rain cleared on her Sunday walk she came to the gate through which she could see the village clustered on the hill across the fields, the sharp triangle of its spire in the centre and the walls and angles and patches of green round the houses gathered to it like a full slack tide. A rain-washed last gleam of the winter afternoon strengthened the light on the buildings, the sky lifting after the rain just before the collection of houses became a hump in the dusk. What perfect timing. What beneficial beauty. 'Ah. Ah,' she breathed, leaning hard against the gate-post, very happy.

There was a piece of flapjack for tea instead of pudding, put out on a plate, one piece each. Before they even sat down, with their mother doling out something hot from a pan in the kitchen, one child picked up a piece and the sweet juiciness of the butter and syrup met with the salivering juices that were overmastering its mouth as it sank its teeth into the thick brown wodge.

It hurt when he swallowed, stabbing with dryness and dust. He felt there were things growing on the back of his throat, closing it up. They had lost their way in the hottest of noons. He was flaring with fever. He would be ill. The glass from the fridge was all misted round with moisture. Beads and trickles of moisture outside and inside the glass. He held his hands round it. Bowing his head he pressed the glass upright against his cheek, his burning forehead. He put his sun-cracked lips against the glass, then up round the thin edge, lifted his head and hand with glass in one movement, and slaked.

The child wanted to go. It couldn't wait. It was in a panic and so was its mother. The child writhed while she asked the attendant.

The corridor was endless. The stairs were worse than the level corridor, moving down the corridor was worse than sitting. The child, clutching moistening pants, was going red in the face holding its breath. They got there. Strangely, for an instant it didn't come. Then the pee came legitimately. 'Oh,' the child breathed and pleasure relaxed its face into a beautiful smile. Oh the relief.

Although he had lowered the window to let the cold wet air refresh him, and breathed it, and moved his neck and shifted his posture and shuddered his skin, his eyes were closing and his head keeling over. He was being overcome. He shuddered and lolled again. He drove on to the verge and parked. He took off his cap and put it over his face, turning sideways away from the road to face the back of the passenger seat. His eyes were still reacting to the prying beams of light that had tired them. Explosions of light burst and ran fluidly on the inside of his eyes. The car rocked as a thundering monster drove past. The noise and vibration was very close but cocooned not alarmed him now. He sank himself through his tiredness as if he were pushing something down through water, concentrating on something beyond, shutting the door behind him. He pushed his face into the inside of his cap up against the firmness of the seat back, nuzzling as if at another, and smelt his hair smell, his warm head smell infinitely pleasurable as if someone's arms were round him, the blanket of sleeping. He took in intentionally the exhalations inside the cap, like a dog. He would not worry about when to wake. He was at the absolute of peace. Pleasure had lifted him there gently, like something lifted above the tide line by a great unbroken quiet wave and laid in safety. He woke after a few minutes and drove to his destination.

Note

As the form of my book *Persephone* developed out of the poem 'Life and Turgid Times of A. Citizen', so *Extended Similes* is further along the line from *Persephone*, being all prose.

The opposition in Persephone was between human predicaments (prose) and the non-human: the gods and goddesses of the old Greek story (verse). The human condition was interpreted in the light of the actions of the 'Gods' i.e. human life v. non-human, with Demeter, of course, on the side of 'her people'.

In *Extended Similes* human situations are presented through descriptions of the natural world. It is the mechanics of human relations that I am trying to get at; so a love affair is told through paragraphs adapted from a car manual about faulty timing ('Out of synch'), the situation of a man living apart from his wife and children described through details of the life of a butterfly ('Butterfly').

The first piece I wrote was 'Extended simile'. I was seeing how far (or how near – how economical) I could go to put the matter that formerly might have gone into a three-volume novel, or recently into a television serial, into a page. As I continued I tried out different sorts of prose rhythms, as well as varying the movement of sentences within a paragraph, and the order and extent of the similes. I also wanted some variety of pace and tone. As in *Persephone*, the juxtapositions provide, I hope, some unwritten enhancing of the writing, as silence between notes in music brings out the sounds.

Whereas *Persephone* was about sex, at one level *Extended Similes* is largely concerned with different aspects of love. Its main ground or terrain is life 'as if': instances of the human being surviving through a variety of ploys, sleights of mind, employed to avoid failure. This is not usually of course a matter of will-power or conscious intent: it is the mechanism implanted in us by the Bitch Goddess Nature to keep us bound upon her wheel and keep that wheel turning.

This is obviously not a work of philosophy, but when I came across Hans Vaihinger's *The Philosophy of 'As if'*, written in 1876 (published in 1911 and translated into English [second edition] by C.K. Ogden, published by Kegan Paul, Trench, Trubner & Co. Ltd in 1935), I thought I had found the book I had been for years thinking I must write and that therefore I needn't go on with mine. Vaihinger writes in his introduction, 'I called this work *The Philosophy of "As if"* because it seemed to me to express more convincingly than any other possible title what I wanted to say, namely that "As if ", i.e. appearance, the consciously false, plays an enormous part in science, in world-philosophies and in life. I wanted to give a complete enumeration of all the methods in which we operate intentionally with consciously false ideas, or rather judgements. I wanted to reveal the secret life of these extraordinary methods. *I wanted to give a complete theory, an anatomy and physiology so to speak, or rather a biology of "As if"*'. (My italics.) Later I found I had to do my book after all.

The presence of Samuel Johnson in the book acknowledges that it was partly a close reading of some of his *Rambler* essays, trying to find out how he got his effects through his particular use of grammatical structure, that led me to noticing his dependence on metaphor and simile (usually associated with poetry) for carrying the meaning of his prose argument. It seems to be carried by the surface logic of the structure of his prose sentences but the line of thought is also developed through his metaphors.

Where I got that perception from I'm afraid has sunk to a currently unreachable layer in the ragbag of my memory, but I'm sure it was originally someone else's. (Apart from liking the name, I always felt kin to Autolycus, that 'snapper-up of unconsidered trifles' in *A Winter's Tale*.) Perhaps I might here include a general appreciation of all the other unacknowledged suppliers of goods that I have used. I am grateful for the word-hoard of our language that is not original to any single one of us but is for the use of all, that increases rather than diminishes with use. What can be more magical and sensible than that?

J.J.

Jenny Joseph was first published by John Lehmann in the 1950s. Her first book of poems, *The Unlooked-for Season* (1960), won her a Gregory Award, and she won a Cholmondeley Award for her second collection, *Rose in the Afternoon* (1974). Two further collections followed from Secker, *The Thinking Heart* (1978) and *Beyond Descartes* (1983). Her *Selected Poems* was published by Bloodaxe in 1992, drawing on these four books. Her latest collection is *Ghosts and Other Company* (Bloodaxe, 1995).

Her other books include: *Persephone* (Bloodaxe, 1986), winner of the James Tait Black Memorial Prize; *Beached Boats* (Enitharmon Press, 1991), a collaboration with photographer Robert Mitchell; and *Extended Similes* (Bloodaxe Books, 1997). She lives in Gloucestershire.